CHATGPT FOR TEACHERS
AND STUDENTS

CRAIG SHIELDS

ChatGPT for Teachers and Students

Disclaimer

This publication is designed to provide accurate and authoritative information in regard to the subject matter covered. It is sold with the understanding that neither the author nor the publisher is engaged in rendering legal, investment, accounting, or other professional services. While the publisher and author have used their best efforts in preparing this book, they make no representations or warranties with respect to the accuracy or completeness of the contents of this book and specifically disclaim any implied warranties of merchantability or fitness for a particular purpose. No warranty may be created or extended by sales representatives or written sales materials. The advice and strategies contained herein may not be suitable for your situation. You should consult with a professional when appropriate. Neither the publisher nor the author shall be liable for any loss of profit or any other commercial damages, including but not limited to special, incidental, consequential, personal, or other damages.

Notes on the Text

No portion of this book has been generated by an AI except where the responses are shown from the AI ChatGPT. No other portions of this book are AI-generated. Responses from ChatGPT are shown as an example of the output generated in response to prompting. Text written by ChatGPT is italicized and is shown as follows: *ChatGPT: This is the way AI-generated text is shown in this book.*

Prompts are formatted as underlined and are shown in this book as follows: prompt= This is an example of a prompt sent to the AI.

An ellipsis indicates that text in a prompt or in the AI-generated response has been truncated for brevity. Truncated text will appear as follows: This is an example of...

Notice and Declaration of Responsibility

The author generated this text in part with GPT-4, OpenAI's large-scale language-generation model. Upon generating draft language, the author reviewed, edited, and revised the language to their own liking and takes ultimate responsibility for the content of this publication.

CONTENTS

1

INTRODUCTION

What is ChatGPT?

The online program ChatGPT at chat.openai.com is an interactive chatbot trained on text from billions of web pages across the internet and created by OpenAI. It can write email responses, answer questions, and have an intelligent conversation on nearly any subject. It can analyze text and provide feedback. It can create outlines, test questions, and lesson plans. It can perform interviews from either side, organize ideas, write essays, answer questions, tell stories and jokes, and even help write computer code. It's extremely flexible.

What is a prompt when using ChatGPT?

The way to interact with ChatGPT is by typing in a question or "prompt". A prompt can be just a few words, a fully formatted question statement with syntax and example responses, or the full text of an essay you would like to have analyzed. The details of creating prompts for an array of use cases will be covered in the Prompts sections of this book.

prompt= I have an oral exam coming up in History class. Our book is Advanced Placement World History: Modern. The exam will cover Period 2. Please assist me with an outline for study and tips on taking an oral exam on this material.

A Basic Prompt pasted into ChatGPT

How does ChatGPT work?

It's a calculator for language. It uses what's known as a large language model to predict the next word it's going to type based on its training data. The model analyzes your request or prompt, then calculates and displays its response.

What is a Large Language Model?

The way I understand it, it's complicated mathematics applied to language. It's a collection of text gathered from billions of web pages across the internet and converted into training data. The training data is used to train the model's parameters. Parameters include mathematical relationships, values, weights, percentages, and variations and are stored in the model's neural network. The model learns associations between words by adjusting its parameters during the training process. During the training process, the text data is converted into tokens. The model learns patterns in the data by learning the relationships between the tokens.

What is a token and how does ChatGPT use them?

A token contains a series of characters, usually a word or a subword. The model sees your request as tokens. The model uses the information and relationships stored in its parameters to predict the probability of the next token it will generate, based on the tokens in your request, and on the context of the tokens it has already generated. It does not know the words or their meanings. It only handles the tokens that represent the words. ChatGPT is not trained to talk or write. It's trained to predict what comes next.

What does GPT stand for?

Generative Pre-Trained Transformer. It's a type of language model developed by OpenAI. *Generative* in that it generates text. *Pre-trained* in that the model was trained on a large amount of text and then fine-tuned on language operations. A *transformer* is a type of neural network architecture used for language generation and translation.

How do I get started using ChatGPT?

You can start by going to the following link: chat.openai.com
    The system may be busy. If so you can try again later. You can also set up an account and try the OpenAI playground.

To set up an account even if ChatGPT is too busy, go to this link: openai.com/api. Click signup and follow the instructions to create an account. Once your account is created you'll have access to both ChatGPT and the Playground - OpenAI API interface at platform.openai.com/playground. See the Playground section for more information about the Playground - OpenAI API.

A Note on Editing and Saving your Prompts

One helpful practice is to type your prompts into Word or a text editor program, or even the email or notes program on your phone, where your prompt can be saved. To use your prompt, just edit, then copy and paste it into the chat input line.

Saving the prompts you create and the response from ChatGPT is a good idea because you'll be able to refer to them later along with the output you received. Another reason is, although OpenAI may store the history of your prompts and responses for you, sometimes the history becomes lost or is unavailable for a period of time.

Another benefit of composing your prompts in Word or another text editor is you'll be able to work with the text in your prompt and revise it as needed before submitting it. When you press enter while editing on the chat input line, the system takes the prompt and starts working on it, whether you've finished writing it or not.

New Chat

Click the New Chat button in the upper left corner to reset the conversation and start a new session. This is helpful when you've tried several variations of a prompt but are still not getting the results you want. ChatGPT uses the previous text above your current chat as a reference for your prompts.

Notes on the Text

No portion of this book has been generated by an AI except where the responses are shown from the AI ChatGPT. No other portions of this book are AI-generated. Responses from ChatGPT are shown as an example of the output generated in response to prompting. Text written by ChatGPT is italicized and is shown as follows: *ChatGPT: This is the way AI-generated text is shown in this book.*

Prompts are formatted as underlined and are shown in this book as follows: prompt= This is an example of a prompt sent to the AI.

An ellipsis indicates that text in a prompt or in the AI-generated response has been truncated for brevity. Truncated text will appear as follows: This is an example of....

Notice and Declaration of Responsibility

The author generated this text in part with GPT-4, OpenAI's large-scale language-generation model. Upon generating draft language, the author reviewed, edited, and revised the language to their own liking and takes ultimate responsibility for the content of this publication.

2

PROMPTS I

At its most basic, a prompt is a question for ChatGPT to answer. The best results come from a prompt that is very specific about what you are looking for. Because the model can be used for virtually anything, it's necessary to narrowly define your request.

Oral Exam Preparation Example

To narrow things down, tell it what you want in plain language and be as descriptive as you can. For example, if you want help preparing for an oral exam in History class, just ask:

prompt= I have an oral exam coming up in History class. Our book is Advanced Placement World History: Modern. The exam will cover Period 2. Please assist me with an outline for study and tips on taking an oral exam on this material.

prompt= I have an oral exam coming up in History class. Our book is Advanced Placement World History: Modern. The exam will cover Period 2. Please assist me with an outline for study and tips on taking an oral exam on this material.

Prompt text pasted into ChatGPT

Type the prompt into the chat.openai.com/chat input line or better yet, paste it in from Word or a text editor or the email or notes program on your phone where you have typed it out and saved it for later use. Note: the word prompt= at the beginning is not required and is optional. It is shown that way in this book for clarity.

Here is the response to the oral exam prompt:

ChatGPT: Study Outline:

1. Key events and developments in the early modern period (1450-1750).

2. The impact of European expansion and colonization on the world.

3. The Scientific Revolution and its effects on society and culture.

4. The Enlightenment and its ideas on politics, society, and religion.

5. The French Revolution and its impact on Europe and the world.

6. The Industrial Revolution and its effects on economics, politics, and society.

Tips for Taking the Oral Exam:

1. Be prepared to discuss and explain key events and developments in detail.

2. Know the major players, causes, and consequences of the events.

3. Be able to connect events and developments to broader themes and patterns in world history.

4. Use specific examples to support your points.

5. Be familiar with maps, charts, and graphs related to the material.

6. Practice speaking clearly and concisely, and be ready to answer follow-up questions.

7. Stay relaxed and confident, and take deep breaths if needed.

You can use the response to get more specific information. Say you know that in the exam there will be an emphasis on the French Revolution. Prompt again:

<u>prompt= Generate 5 potential oral exam questions on point 5 in the outline above.</u>

ChatGPT:

1. What were the main causes of the French Revolution?

2. How did the French Revolution impact the political, social, and economic structures of France?

3. Who were the key leaders and thinkers of the French Revolution?

4. How did the ideas and events of the French Revolution influence other countries and events in world history?

5. What were some of the major reforms and changes introduced during the French Revolution, and how did they affect the French people?

Now you have specific information that includes potential test questions over the material you expect to be in the exam.

Classify Items by Example

The example above illustrates telling the model what you want. You can also show it what you want by providing an example of the output you expect to see. Usually, the system can format things well without examples, like a multiple-choice test or a true-false quiz. But you may have a special use case where you'll need to specify how you want the output to appear. Look at this example:

prompt= This is a list of numbers. Identify the prime numbers as shown in the example:

1,2,3,4,5,6,7.
2: Two is a Prime Number.

The prompt contains an example of how you want the response formatted. Here is the response from the system:

ChatGPT:

1: One is not a prime number.

2: Two is a Prime Number.

3: Three is a Prime Number.

4: Four is not a Prime Number.

5: Five is a Prime Number.

6: Six is not a Prime Number.

7: Seven is a Prime Number.

ChatGPT formatted the response as specified in the example from the prompt.

Compare and Contrast Characters with Variables

Another way to tell ChatGPT what you want is by creating custom variables in your prompt. This makes it easy to design a prompt for a specific use and reuse it later. Using custom variables that you create and parameters with numeric values are covered extensively in the Prompts II section of this book.

Here we'll design a prompt to compare characters from two different novels:

prompt=Compare and contrast the character development of [wCharacter] in [xNovel] with [yCharacter] in [zNovel]
    wCharacter=White Fang
    xNovel=White Fang
    yCharacter=Buck
    zNovel=Call of the Wild
    scholarly=70%

Compare and contrast the character development of [wCharacter] in [xNovel] with [yCharacter] in [zNovel]
wCharacter=White Fang
xNovel=White Fang
yCharacter=Buck
zNovel=Call of the Wild
scholarly=70%

Image of prompt text as pasted into ChatGPT

The variables in brackets can be replaced with the characters and novels in question just by typing them after the variable name and = sign at the end of the prompt as shown above. You'll notice I put in a parameter at the end, scholarly=70%, that isn't shown or "declared" in the prompt above, but it still works anyway. It's easy to use parameters like that with numeric values to have a strong influence on the output. Again, more on using variables and parameters in the Prompts II section of this book.

. . .

Here is the output from ChatGPT for our character development prompt:

ChatGPT: White Fang, the main character in Jack London's novel "White Fang," is a wolf-dog hybrid who lives in the harsh environment of the Klondike during the late 1800s. Throughout the course of the novel, White Fang experiences a transformation from a wild and ferocious animal to a domesticated and loyal pet. This change is brought about by his interactions with humans, particularly with the novel's protagonist, a gold hunter named Weedon Scott.

Buck, the main character in Jack London's novel "Call of the Wild," is a domesticated dog who is taken from his comfortable life in California and thrust into the harsh world of the Klondike gold rush. Over the course of the novel, Buck becomes increasingly wild and feral as he is forced to adapt to the brutal conditions of the Yukon. He eventually becomes the leader of a pack of wolves, embracing his inner wildness and discovering his true nature as a wild animal.

Both characters undergo significant changes throughout the course of their respective novels, but the direction of those changes is the opposite. While White Fang becomes more domesticated and civilized, Buck becomes more wild and feral. This contrast can be seen as a reflection of the themes of civilization vs. nature and the duality of human and animal nature that are present in both novels.

Recap

So to recap prompting so far:

Tell the system what you want. Be specific.

Show the system what you want with examples if necessary.

You can create variables as placeholders in your prompt and define them at the end.

You can modify the response using parameters with numeric values.

In the OpenAI Playground section, the playground interface is described and the parameters shown there are discussed.

3

PLAYGROUND - OPENAI API

What is the Playground - OpenAI API interface?

It's similar to ChatGPT in that you'll type in your prompt or question and when you click submit, the model will give a response. But there are some differences:

- The playground uses a slightly different model than ChatGPT, text-davinci-003, by default.
- The playground has on-screen parameters that you can change to modify its response.
- The window to input your prompt is larger than the normal ChatGPT interface.
- It's not free, but you get a credit when you sign up, which will last a LONG time if you aren't sending or receiving large amounts of data, see below. Please see the OpenAI site for current costs.
- The Playground - OpenAI API interface is primarily designed for testing API access and

allows using any of the models that OpenAI offers. Each of the models has different costs.

At any time if you want to use the standard ChatGPT site just click the button at the bottom of the page to go there. Many times, the playground site will be available while ChatGPT is too busy.

How do I go to the Playground - OpenAI API Interface?

To log in and access the playground, go to platform.openai.com/playground and log in.

Is the Playground - OpenAI API Interface Free?

Unlike ChatGPT, which, at this time, has both free and paid options where the tokens you use are not billed, access to the models on the Playground - OpenAI API interface is not free and it is metered in tokens. When you sign up as a free trial user, at this time, your account is automatically granted a credit which you are free to use in the Playground - OpenAI API interface. This credit is used for tokens. Please see the OpenAI site for the current costs for the various models.

For example, the use of 1,000 tokens for the gpt-3.5-turbo model costs $0.0020 at the time of this writing, March 2023. So a $5.00 grant is worth about 2,500,000 tokens. 1,500 words are worth about 2,048 tokens. So a $5.00 grant is worth about 1,800,000 words. Again, please see the OpenAI site for current information on costs associated with their services.

Playground - OpenAI API Interface

In the Playground - OpenAI API interface on the right edge of the screen, there are several parameters you can adjust. A few of those parameters will be covered here.

Top Right - Playground - OpenAI API

Starting at the top right and going down the right-hand side, these are the options:

Load a preset... - Has example settings that can be used for special cases. Also has a link to the examples page.

Save - Save your custom settings and place the name you select into the load preset list.

View Code - This opens a window to display the computer code of your request. This can be very helpful because it shows exactly what is being sent to the model to process.

Share - This allows you to send a link to someone to share the preset you have saved.

... - Allows you to turn off the warning for unsafe content.

.   .   .

Still on the right side at the top, below the view code button, you'll see the word **Mode** and 4 options under it (March 2023 update). To change from one to the other, just click it once. The options are:

Mode options dropdown

Complete - This is the default mode for the playground window. The window is set up for you to type your prompt and receive your completion in the center window.

Chat (Beta) - Sets up the playground window to allow a system command and a user command to control a chat session.

Insert (Beta) - Place the code [insert] in your prompt where the model should insert its response. The response will include your prompt with the model's completion text located at the point where the [insert] code occurs. For example... prompt: Opening of a form letter... [insert].... Closing of the form letter (end of your prompt), where the body of the letter is being supplied by the model.

Edit (Beta) - Allows you to provide instructions to the model on how it should edit your prompt, for example, fix the grammar for the text you have submitted.

Model Options

These are the GPT-3 options that the playground makes available for you to use. The text-davinci-003 model is the most recent and is the default option for the playground interface. For teachers and students, for general use, davinci is the best choice.

Model	
text-davinci-003	
Temperature	0.7
Maximum length	256
Stop sequences	
Top P	1
Frequency penalty	0
Presence penalty	0

Model and Parameters

text-davinci-003 - Best overall choice, follows instructions well, long output, high quality.

text-curie-001 - Runs faster and at a lower cost than davinci, but is somewhat less capable.

text-babbage-001 - Very fast, low cost, best for simpler tasks.

text-ada-001 - Lowest cost and fastest of the GPT-3 models.

There are other model options listed. These are older

models that would only be used if you have a special case that requires using an older version of a current model. The Codex models are designed for working with computer code. The GPT-4 model is available in the playground - OpenAI API interface on a waitlist basis. Using the regular ChatGPT at chat.openai.com is the best way to gain access to the GPT-4 model for anyone who is not programming and working with the API interface.

Parameters in the Playground - OpenAI API interface

The values shown below are the default parameters when you open the Playground - OpenAI API interface. It is also possible to specify custom values for these parameters when working with the ChatGPT interface. Please see the Prompts II chapter for more information.

Temperature= Default value is .7, with a range from 0 to 1. It controls the level of randomness in the generated text. A setting of zero will adhere very closely to the prompt you give the system with very little in the way of creativity or improvisation. Higher numbers will introduce more randomness in the calculation of the response and generate a more creative output. Zero is no surprises, 1 will contain the most varied, innovative, and creative replies. Play around with the value for Temperature: and notice the effect it has on the completion of your prompt.

Maximum_length= This controls how many tokens the system could potentially use in its reply. The default value is 256 which is usually fine if your expected reply is less than a few hundred words. The maximum value is about 4,000 tokens, which is shared between the prompt and comple-tion. Setting this to a value above 2,000 will begin to limit the amount of input the system will accept from your prompt.

Stop sequences: Used for programming with the API to stop output.

Top_P= Default value is 1. The range is from 0 to 1. A setting of 0 means the model will consider a larger number of possible tokens for its response. The lower setting results in more variance and creativity in the response at the cost of a higher likelihood of errors or incorrect information. A setting of 1 means that the model will consider a smaller number of more likely tokens. The higher setting inclines the model to produce more accurate and conservative text but at the cost of creativity. This setting operates in conjunction with the Temperature setting. Temperature controls the randomness, and Top_P controls how certain the model is when predicting what tokens to use in its response.

Frequency_penalty= and **Presence_penalty=** Default value is 0. The range is from 0 to 1. Both penalize new tokens based on the tokens that have been used so far. Raising the value of frequency_penalty decreases the probability that the system will repeat a line. Raising the value of presence_penalty increases the probability that the response will contain new topics.

Skipping down to the bottom right of the Playground - OpenAI API interface, there is a number just to the left of the "Show probabilities" option. This number shows the number of tokens used in your prompt so far. This number updates as you type.

Token Counter

Finally, the Submit button is at the bottom left along with icons for remove last response, regenerate response, and show history. The link for ChatGPT is also shown here.

Lower Left Submit, Remove, Regen, History

To use the Playground - OpenAI API interface, simply type your prompt into the large window in the center and click the submit button at the lower left to generate the response.

Some of the parameters listed above can also be used in ChatGPT. See the Prompts I and II sections of this book for more information.

. . .

It bears mentioning that supplying these parameters to ChatGPT is not the same as supplying a parameter to a model in the Playground - OpenAI API interface. In the Playground - OpenAI API interface, the model takes the parameter as one of its startup variables and runs using the value supplied. ChatGPT is already running the startup parameters supplied by OpenAI. ChatGPT understands parameters if they are given in a prompt and it takes them as a suggestion that it will use during its calculations, but the parameter is not part of its initial processing of the response to your request.

4

PROMPTS II AND CUSTOM VARIABLES

The Power of Language in the Prompt

The wording of a prompt has a profound effect on the response from the system. Let's try a creative writing example. First, we'll ask ChatGPT to write a paragraph about a spring flower garden. Then we'll add the phrase "very descriptive" and note the results.

Creative Writing 1

prompt= Write a paragraph about a spring flower garden.

ChatGPT: A spring flower garden is a sight to behold. As winter comes to an end and temperatures start to rise, the garden comes alive with a vibrant array of blooms. From delicate cherry blossom trees to brightly colored tulips and daffodils, the garden is awash with color and fragrance. Visitors can stroll through the garden, taking in the beauty and peace of nature. Whether it is a public park or a private backyard, a spring flower garden is a symbol of hope and renewal, reminding us that even after the darkest days, there is always new life and beauty to be found.

Creative Writing 2 + Adjectives

prompt= Write a very descriptive paragraph about a spring flower garden.

ChatGPT: A spring flower garden is a kaleidoscope of colors, scents, and textures. Rows of tulips in shades of pink, red, and yellow sway gently in the breeze, their delicate petals kissed by the sun. A riot of daffodils, with their bright yellow cups and green stems, blanket the ground in a cheerful carpet. The sweet fragrance of lilacs fills the air, as their clusters of purple blooms nod in the breeze. Peonies, in soft hues of pink and white, add a touch of grace and elegance. Butterflies flit from flower to flower, their wings a blur of iridescent color. Amidst the flowers, the buzz of busy bees can be heard as they collect nectar. The spring flower garden is a symphony of life and beauty.

Creative Writing 3 + Include Words

The big difference between those two paragraphs illustrates the power of language in the prompt. In this case, we gave a command and told the system what we wanted but left it up to ChatGPT what to say exactly. I have experimented with adding descriptive phrases to the prompt. It will use these supplied phrases at the price of some creativity. It may even repeat those specified words. Here is an example:

prompt= Write a paragraph about a spring flower garden. Include the words imaginative, whimsical, and exotic.

ChatGPT: A spring flower garden is a place where imagination, whimsy, and exotic beauty come to life. As the flowers begin to bloom, the garden is transformed into a colorful and fragrant wonderland. The imaginative arrangements of the flowers, with their whimsical shapes and patterns, create a peaceful and dreamlike atmosphere. The exotic blooms, with their unique colors and shapes, add to the garden's already breathtaking beauty, making it a perfect escape from the mundane world. Whether you're admiring the beauty or simply taking a stroll, a spring flower garden is sure to leave a lasting impression.

Creative Writing 4 + Avoid Repeating

Notice that the included words are repeated several times each. An effective way to work around that is to ask it to not repeat the included words as follows:

prompt= Write a paragraph about a spring flower garden. Include the words imaginative, whimsical, and exotic without repeating them.

ChatGPT: A spring flower garden is a tapestry of colors, shapes, and scents woven together in an imaginative way. The blossoms in a whimsical dance with the breeze, displaying their exotic beauty to all who dare to stop and admire. This garden is a place where one can escape reality and be transported to a world of wonder and enchantment, surrounded by the most delicate and unique flowers from far-off lands. Here, the imagination is sparked, the senses are invigorated, and the soul is renewed.

So, it only repeated one form of imaginative which is an improvement over the previous sample.

Creative Writing 5 + Using Required Words as Commands

Another example, this time we'll use the required words as part of the command.

<u>prompt= Write an imaginative, whimsical, and exotic paragraph about a spring flower garden.</u>

ChatGPT: A spring flower garden was a place of magic and wonder, where colorful blooms of tulips, daffodils, and hyacinths danced in the gentle breeze. Butterflies flitted from flower to flower, while the sweet fragrance of jasmine and roses filled the air. It was a place where fairies might gather to play and where a unicorn might pause to drink from a crystal clear stream. The sun shone down upon the garden, warming the petals and casting a golden glow upon everything it touched. It was a place of enchantment, a place of peace, a place of beauty beyond compare.

Again, the language in the prompt shapes the output. Not sure why it switched to past tense. Probably due to the random nature of the responses that ChatGPT generates.

Using Parameters

Another way to influence the output is by using parameters. The parameters we'll see here are temperature, top_p, frequency_penalty, presence_penalty, and max_tokens. These parameters have less of an effect on the output than the language in the prompt. The last, maximum_length, controls how long the response will be.

Temperature - Range is from zero to one. Controls the

level of randomness in the generated text. A setting of zero will adhere very closely to the prompt you provided with very little in the way of creativity or improvisation. Higher numbers will introduce more randomness in the calculation of the response and generate a more creative output.

Top_P - The range for this parameter is from zero to one. A setting of 0 means the model will consider a larger number of possible tokens for its response. The lower setting results in more variance and creativity in the response at the cost of a higher likelihood of errors or incorrect information. A setting of 1 means that the model will consider a smaller number of more likely tokens. The higher setting inclines the model to produce more accurate and conservative text but at the cost of creativity. This setting operates in conjunction with the Temperature setting. Temperature controls the randomness, and Top_P controls how certain the model is when predicting what tokens to use in its response.

Frequency_penalty and **Presence_penalty** - The range for these parameters is from zero to one. Both penalize new tokens based on the tokens that have been used so far. Raising the value of frequency_penalty decreases the probability that the system will repeat a line. Raising the value of presence_penalty increases the probability that the response will contain new topics.

Max_tokens This controls how many tokens the system could potentially use in its reply. See the OpenAI beta Playground section for a full description of tokens. One token equals about 4 characters. Change this setting to limit the length of the response from ChatGPT.

.   .   .

To use a parameter in a prompt, add the parameter as the last line.

Using top_p

Here's an example from above with top_p=0 added as a parameter. This is telling ChatGPT to consider a larger number of tokens for its response than it normally would.

prompt= Write a paragraph about a spring flower garden.
top_p=0

ChatGPT: A spring flower garden is a feast for the senses, with a kaleidoscope of colors, fragrances and textures. As the snow melts and the soil warms, delicate blooms burst forth, bringing life and joy to the garden. From the pastel pinks and purples of blooming cherry trees, to the bright yellows and oranges of daffodils and tulips, the spring flower garden is a tapestry of beauty. The air is filled with the sweet fragrance of hyacinths and lilacs, and the buzz of bees as they gather nectar from the flowers. Whether you stroll through the garden or simply sit and enjoy the view, a spring flower garden is a true delight.

The use of top_p seems to have brought in a few more elements than our original example above but without the location or the theme of spring renewal. The effects of these parameters are difficult to judge due to the subtle nature of the adjustments. Experiment with them in combinations if you're looking for variations in the output of the system.

Using top_p + max_tokens

Here is an example of limiting the length of the response using maximum_length:

prompt= Write a paragraph about a spring flower garden.
top_p=0
max_tokens=20
ChatGPT: A spring flower garden is a colorful and fragrant display of blooming flowers such as tulips, daffodils, crocuses and hyacinths. The garden provides a vibrant atmosphere and is a popular destination for visitors and photographers alike.

That response is about half the size of the last one, showing the limit imposed by max_tokens.

The above parameters are interesting to experiment with, especially if you're looking for a certain feeling in the text output that you're not getting.

Using Custom Variables - Interviewer and Interviewee

Because ChatGPT is a computer program, it is possible to communicate with it like a computer program. This opens up the possibility to create your own variables and templates that you can use over and over. Just create and save a text prompt with variables one time and adjust the output from the system for different situations by changing only the variables. It's easier and faster than rewording the entire prompt. Here is an example text prompt template:

. . .

prompt= You are now an interviewer. You will ask one question at a time and wait for my answer before asking another question. [interviewer type] is the kind of interviewer you are. [Interviewee type] is the kind of interviewee I am. The purpose of the interview is [purpose]. Use the following [information] as the basis for your questions. I begin the interview by greeting you with "Hello". Please ask your first question.

interviewer type=
    interviewee type=
    purpose=
    information=

This prompt tells ChatGPT that it is now an interviewer. It's instructed to ask one question at a time and wait for the response before asking another question. We are telling ChatGPT about the situation using the variables [interviewer_type], [interviewee_type], [purpose], and additional information with [information]. Finally, we instruct ChatGPT that it has received a greeting and to ask its first question.

To use this prompt, we must type in the information at the bottom after the = sign for each item and paste the prompt into the ChatGPT interface.

Let's say we want to practice for an oral exam in History and we know the focus will be on the French Revolution. I'll fill in the variables as follows:

. . .

interviewer_type= College History Teacher

interviewee_type= College History Student

purpose= You're asking questions for an oral exam in History.

information= Focus the questions on the French Revolution.

Notice that there are underscores instead of spaces between words in the variables. Here is the prompt as submitted and some of the responses:

prompt= You are now an interviewer. You will ask one question at a time and wait for my answer before asking another question. [interviewer type] is the kind of interviewer you are. [Interviewee type] is the kind of interviewee I am. The purpose of the interview is [purpose]. Use the following [information] as the basis for your questions. I begin the interview by greeting you with "Hello". Please ask your first question.

interviewer type= College History Teacher

interviewee type= College History Student

purpose= You're asking questions for an oral exam in History.

information= Focus the questions on the French Revolution.

ChatGPT: Hello, can you briefly describe the causes of the French Revolution?

Interviewee
Causes of the French revolution include...

ChatGPT: What was the role of the Estate System in the French Revolution?
Interviewee
The role of the Estate System...

ChatGPT: How did the ideas of the Enlightenment influence the French Revolution?

We can see that ChatGPT started asking questions about the French Revolution as requested. This template can be reused for other subjects and situations. You can be the interviewer or the subject of the interview. It's very flexible.

Creative Writing with Custom Variables + Numeric Values

You can also use custom variables to change the character of the output text. Let's try one with the garden prompt from earlier:

prompt= Write a paragraph about a spring flower garden.
    imaginative=1
    whimsical=1
    exotic=1
    ChatGPT: A spring flower garden is a whimsical, exotic wonderland. The air is filled with the sweet fragrance of blooming

flowers in every color of the rainbow. The sun shines down upon the garden, illuminating the vibrant petals and creating a mesmerizing dance of light and shadow. The flowers sway gently in the breeze, their delicate stems bending and twisting, as if they are performing a graceful ballet. In this magical place, time seems to stand still, and one can escape from the hustle and bustle of everyday life. The flowers seem to come alive, their petals opening and closing, inviting visitors to come closer and admire their beauty. It's a place where the impossible becomes possible, where fantasy and reality blend together, and where one can simply sit back, relax, and bask in the joy of spring.

It works similarly to including the words in the command. Let's try turning the values down to 0.2 (20%) and see what happens:

prompt= Write a paragraph about a spring flower garden.
    imaginative=0.2
    whimsical=0.2
    exotic=0.2

ChatGPT: A spring flower garden is a picturesque and colorful display of nature's beauty. With the arrival of spring, the garden comes to life with a variety of flowers in bloom. From fragrant lilacs to bright tulips, the garden is a delight for the senses. The exotic blooms of peonies and the whimsical shapes of daffodils add to the charm of the garden, making it a perfect place for a peaceful stroll or a picnic with friends.

Setting the values to 0.2 (20%) definitely turned down the effect of those words on the text. Using variables with numeric values gives a fine control that isn't possible by simply including the words in the prompt as we did earlier.

For the values of your variables, a percentage, like 90%, works as well as a decimal value. Use whatever you are most comfortable with. Try this example:

prompt= Write a paragraph about a spring flower garden.
    imaginative=90%
    whimsical=90%
    exotic=90%

ChatGPT: A spring flower garden is a whimsical, exotic, and imaginative feast for the senses. The blooms come alive with their own personalities, each one more enchanting than the next. The tulips sway to the rhythm of an unheard song, while the peonies hold court like regal queens. The daffodils giggle in the breeze, as the lilacs release their sweet fragrance into the air. It's as if the garden has its own secret world, filled with fantastical creatures and mystical blooms. The vivid colors, intriguing scents, and imaginative beauty of this wondrous place will leave you spellbound.

The possibilities are nearly endless when making up your own variables. Experiment! It can't possibly break anything and it's a lot of fun. Invent your own variables, save the prompt, and reuse it over and over.

The Top 10 Most Powerful Words and Phrases for Learning with ChatGPT

1. **"In detail"** or **"Step by step"**: Ask for a comprehensive, step-by-step explanation.
2. **"Pros and cons"**: A balanced view, considering both the positive and negative aspects of a topic.
3. **"Critically analyze"** or **"Evaluate"**: Prompts the AI to assess a subject more thoroughly, considering different perspectives and evidence.
4. **"Explain like I'm [age/role/expertise level/lexile level]"**: Tailors the response to a specific audience, making the explanation more accessible or advanced, as needed.
5. **"Provide examples"** or **"Illustrate with case studies"**: Encourages the AI to include real-life examples or case studies to support its explanation.
6. **"Compare and contrast"**: Analyze the similarities and differences between two or more concepts or ideas.
7. **"Key takeaways"** or **"Summary"**: Distill the essential points or conclusions from a topic.
8. **"Best practices"** or **"Effective strategies"**: Provide practical advice or proven methods to address a problem or achieve a goal.
9. **"Discuss the implications"** or **"Consequences"**: Explore the potential outcomes or impacts of a decision, action, or event.
10. **"Historical context"** or **"Background"**: Requests the AI to consider the historical background or

context of a topic, providing a more well-rounded understanding.

Combine these words and phrases with the parameter technique discussed earlier in this book for even more creative and interesting results. Here is an example based on the creative writing exercise from earlier in this book:

prompt= Write a paragraph about a spring flower garden. Imaginative=90%   Whimsical=90%   Exotic=90% Detailed=100%

ChatGPT, Model GPT-4: In the heart of the Enchanted Azuria, a breathtaking spring flower garden flourishes, where petals pirouette to the symphony of a whimsical zephyr. This magical haven, abundant with vivid, exotic flora, is home to the rarest and most fantastical species. The blossoming Trillium Fantasia sway like graceful ballerinas in fuchsia, teal, and gold, while the hypnotic swirls of the Spiralina Orchids beckon visitors into a mesmerizing, chromatic waltz. Here, a cascade of iridescent petals from the ever-glowing Moonlit Lilies illuminate the nightscape, bathing the garden in a celestial luminescence. In this ethereal paradise, the air is imbued with the intoxicating fragrance of the Elysian Plumeria, a scent said to evoke a euphoric sense of serenity. As one strolls along the meandering cobblestone paths, lined with delicate crystal sculptures, the enchantment of this exquisite spring flower garden is forever etched upon the soul, a vivid, transcendent reminder of nature's boundless wonder.

5

EXAMPLE PROMPTS

1. Flashcards - Interactive Practice using a Defined List.

prompt= You are now a flash card reviewer. You will read one question at a time from the supplied [list] and wait for my answer. If my answer does not equal the supplied answer say "incorrect" before reading the answer to the question. You will then say "Next Question" and read the next question and wait for my answer. Please read the first question.

list=

Question: What year was the first train equipped with air brakes?

Answer: 1869

Question: What year did George Westinghouse and Nikola Tesla begin collaboration?

Answer: 1888

Question: Did the Westinghouse Air Brake Company ever experience a strike?

Answer: No

. . .

ChatGPT: Next Question: What year was the first train equipped with air brakes?

prompt=1869
ChatGPT: Correct!

ChatGPT: Next Question: What year did George Westinghouse and Nikola Tesla begin collaboration?

prompt= 1888
ChatGPT: Correct!

ChatGPT: Next Question: Did the Westinghouse Air Brake Company ever experience a strike?

prompt= no
ChatGPT: Correct!

2. Summarize a text for an X-grade level student.

prompt= Summarize this text for a third-grade student:
The Moon travels around Earth in an oval orbit at 3680 kilometers per hour. The Moon does not have an atmosphere, so temperatures range from -184 degrees Celsius during its night to 214 degrees Celsius during its day except at the poles where the temperature is a constant -96 degrees Celsius. The Moon is actually...

ChatGPT: The Moon goes around Earth really fast and is a big rock. It's really hot during the day and really cold at night. It's kind of uneven on one side. There's light parts and dark parts on the Moon. The dark parts are flat places called maria, and the light parts are like mountains. The dark parts were made when a big rock hit it, and the light parts were made when other big rocks hit it.

3. Use TL;DR to Summarize a Text Sample.

prompt= Voyager 2, a space probe, passed within 4900 kilometers of Neptune in 1989. From the data collected, we know that Uranus and Neptune are very similar in composition. Neptune has a mantle of liquid hydrogen while the atmosphere is a combination of ammonia, helium, and methane. In the upper atmosphere, methane freezes and forms an ice cloud which casts a shadow on the clouds below. Neptune has bands in its atmosphere where wind speeds may reach 2000 kilometers per hour! Neptune has large, dark ovals on its surface which astronomers believe are hurricane-like storms. Neptune generates more heat than it absorbs from the Sun, indicating it has its own internal heat source.
   TL;DR

ChatGPT: Voyager 2 passed Neptune in 1989, revealing that it has a mantle of liquid hydrogen and atmosphere composed of ammonia, helium, and methane, with ice clouds and high-speed winds. It has dark ovals on its surface believed to be storm systems and generates more heat than it receives from the sun indicating an internal heat source.

4. Turn Meeting Notes into a Summary.

prompt= Turn my shorthand notes into a first-hand narrative of the short story meeting:
   AJ: Read but didn't like.

TC: Forgot to.
BR: Last week story better.
AJ: Agrees. Likes author.
LM: Read wrong story. Ok.

ChatGPT: At the short story meeting, AJ shared that they had read a story but didn't like it. TC admitted they forgot to read the story, BR mentioned that they thought the story from the previous week was better. AJ agreed with BR's opinion and added that they liked the author of the story discussed today. LM mentioned that they had read the wrong story, but it was okay.

5. Get Keywords from the Supplied Text.

prompt= Extract the keywords from the following text:

The 2022-2023 high school debate topic is: Resolved: The United States federal government should substantially increase its security cooperation with the North Atlantic Treaty Organization in one or more of the following areas: artificial intelligence, biotechnology, cybersecurity. The topic is selected annually by ballot of the delegates from the National Catholic Forensic League, the National Debate Coaches Association, and the National Speech and Debate Association, all organized under the umbrella organization, the National Federation of State High School Associations.

ChatGPT: 2022-2023, high school, debate topic, United States, federal government, security cooperation, North Atlantic Treaty Organization, artificial intelligence, biotechnology, cybersecurity, ballot, delegates, National Catholic Forensic League, National Debate Coaches Association, National Speech and Debate Associ-

ation, umbrella organization, National Federation of State High School Associations.

6. Create a Three-column Spreadsheet in .csv Format.

<u>prompt= Create a three-column spreadsheet of the last names of all United States Presidents, the Year Elected, the Year they left office:</u>
    <u>Last Name, Year Elected, Year Left Office</u>

ChatGPT: I'm sorry, but I'm not able to create spreadsheets. However, I can provide you with the information you need to fill out the spreadsheet. (ChatGPT sometimes claims inability to do a task before doing the task.) *Here is a list of the last names of all United States Presidents, the year they were elected, and the year they left office:*

Washington, 1789, 1797
   Adams, 1797, 1801
   Jefferson, 1801, 1809
   ...
   Trump, 2017, 2021
   Biden, 2021, incumbent

7. Explain a Piece of Python Code.

<u>prompt=</u>
   <u># python</u>
   <u>try:</u>
   <u>number = int(input("Type a number: "))</u>
   <u>if number % 2 == 0:</u>

```
print("Number is even")
else:
print("Number is odd")
except (ValueError):
# Print error message
print("Enter a number value")
#Explanation of what this code does
```

ChatGPT: This code is a python script that prompts the user to input a number and then checks whether it is even or odd. The input is first obtained by calling the input() function and passing in the string "Type a number: ". The input obtained is then...

8. Create an Analogy for a Phrase.

prompt= Please create an analogy for the following phrase:
A cow heading for the barn is like

ChatGPT: A ship heading for port. Both are moving towards a specific destination after a journey.

9. Correct the Grammar of the Submitted Text.

prompt= Correct the language of the following sentence:
I could care less about a extra space.

ChatGPT: I couldn't care less about an extra space.

10. Extract Specified Information from a Block of Text.

prompt= Extract the URLs from the following text:

Artificial intelligence : background, selected issues, and policy considerations

Available   at: https://purl.fdlp.gov/GPO/gpo174251
Publisher: Congressional Research Service

Year: 2021-

Print price: N/A

Available   at: https://purl.fdlp.gov/GPO/gpo177875
Publisher: United States Government Accountability Office
Years/Pages: 2022; iii, 83 pages

Print price: N/A

Assessing the value of the NATO alliance

Available   at: https://purl.fdlp.gov/GPO/gpo140280
Publisher: U.S. Government Publishing Office Year/Pages: 2020; iii, 58 pages

Print price: N/A

ChatGPT: https://purl.fdlp.gov/GPO/gpo174251
   https://purl.fdlp.gov/GPO/gpo177875
   https://purl.fdlp.gov/GPO/gpo140280

11. Translate Supplied Text into Other Languages.

prompt= Translate this sentence into A. German, B. Portuguese, and C. Dutch:

What time does the next bus arrive?

ChatGPT:
   A. German: Wann kommt der nächste Bus an?

B. Portuguese: Que horas o próximo ônibus chega?

C. Dutch: Wanneer komt de volgende bus aan?

12. Write a Research Topic Outline.

prompt= Create an outline for an informational essay about NATO.

ChatGPT: I. Introduction

A. Definition of NATO (North Atlantic Treaty Organization)

B. Brief history of NATO

C. Purpose of NATO

II. Membership

A. Current member states

B. Membership requirements

C. Membership benefits

III. Military Structure and Operations

A. Military command structure

B. Defence spending

C. Past and current military operations

D. Relationship with the United Nations

IV. Political and Economic Cooperation

A. Political cooperation among member states

B. Economic cooperation among member states

C. Cooperation with non-member states

. . .

V. Criticisms and Controversies

    A. Criticisms of NATO's military actions

    B. Criticisms of NATO's political and economic policies

    C. Controversies surrounding NATO's relationship with other countries and organizations

VI. Conclusion

    A. Recap of main points

    B. Importance of NATO in current international relations

    C. Potential future developments for NATO.

13. Classify Supplied Items by Showing an Example.

prompt= This is a list of words and the part of speech they belong to:

    WOW!, Angry, Toad, Run, They, Quickly, And, Until

    WOW! is an: Interjection

ChatGPT:

    Angry: Adjective

    Toad: Noun

    Run: Verb

    They: Pronoun

    Quickly: Adverb

    And: Conjunction

    Until: Conjunction

14. Get Bullet Points limited by max_tokens.

prompt= What are 5 bullet points about snow?

    max_tokens=100

<u>temperature=0.2</u>

ChatGPT: 1. Snow is a form of precipitation that forms when water vapor freezes into ice crystals in the atmosphere.

2. Snow can come in different forms, such as flakes, granules, and pellets.

3. Snowpack formed by accumulating snowfall can be an important water resource.

4. Snow has insulating properties and reflects sunlight, affecting temperature and albedo.

5. Snowfall can affect human activities and wildlife, and climate change is expected to alter snow patterns.

15. Write a List of Interview Questions.

<u>prompt= Write a list of 5 interview questions for a college math professor.</u>

ChatGPT: 1. Can you tell us about your educational background and how you became a math professor?

2. Can you describe your research interests and current projects?

3. How do you approach teaching mathematics to college students?

4. How do you involve and encourage undergraduate students to participate in research opportunities?

5. Can you discuss any initiatives or programs you have implemented to improve math education at the college level?

16. Convert Supplied Text from First Person to Third Person.

prompt= Convert this from first person to third person (gender male):
    I started working on the machine. It was dirty, so I cleaned it.

ChatGPT: He started working on the machine. It was dirty, so he cleaned it.

17. True/False Quiz with an Answer Key.

prompt= You are a school teacher of 3rd-grade science who is testing the knowledge of their students with a true/false quiz on the topic of 'Weather'. Write the quiz, include 8 questions, include at least one question where the correct answer is 'false'. Place the answer key at the end of the quiz.

ChatGPT: Weather Quiz for 3rd-Grade Students
    1. True or False: The sun causes the wind to blow.
    2. True or False: Lightning is hot.
    3. True or False: A rainbow is formed when light is refracted through water droplets in the air.
    4. True or False: Rain only falls from clouds when they are dark and grey.
    5. True or False: Thunder is the noise made by lightning.
    6. True or False: The temperature is the same inside and outside of a cloud.
    7. True or False: Clouds are made of solid matter.

8. True or False: Hurricanes are only found in the Atlantic Ocean.

Answer Key:

1. False

2. True

3. True

4. False

5. True

6. False

7. False

8. False

18. Multiple-choice Quiz with an Answer Key.

prompt= You are a school teacher of 3rd-grade geography who is testing the knowledge of their students with a multiple choice quiz on the topic of 'continents'. Write the quiz, include 5 questions with 3 choices each. Place the answer key at the end of the quiz.

ChatGPT: Quiz: Continents

1. Which continent is the smallest?

a) Africa

b) Europe

c) Antarctica

2. Which continent has the highest population?

a) Asia

b) North America

c) South America

3. Which continent is the largest?

a) Europe

b) Asia

c) Africa

4. Which continent is home to the longest mountain range, the Andes?

a) North America

b) South America

c) Africa

5. Which continent is the only continent that does not have a desert?

a) Antarctica

b) Europe

c) Australia

Answer Key:

1. c

2. a

3. b

4. b

5. b

19. Fill-in-the-blanks Quiz with an Answer Key.

prompt= You are a school teacher of 3rd grade English who is testing the knowledge of their students with a fill-in-the-blank quiz on the topic of 'The eight parts of speech'. Write the quiz, include 5 questions. Place the answer key at the end of the quiz.

ChatGPT: 1. The word "happy" is a/an _____.

2. The word "to" is a/an _____.

3. The word "dog" is a/an _____.

4. The phrase "I am" is a/an _____.

5. The word "run" is a/an _____.

Answer Key:

1. adjective

2. preposition

3. noun

4. verb

5. verb

20. 5-question Factual Answer Quiz with an Answer Key.

prompt= You are a high school teacher of 11th-grade Literature who is testing the knowledge of their students with a short factual answer quiz on the topic of 'Shakespeare plays'. Make the questions medium difficulty. Do not include material about Romeo and Juliet or Hamlet. Write the quiz, include 5 questions. Place the answer key at the end of the quiz.

ChatGPT: 1. In what year did Shakespeare write "Macbeth"?

2. Who is the tragic hero in "Othello"?

3. What is the setting of "The Tempest"?

4. In "King Lear", what are the names of Lear's three daughters?

5. What is the name of the play in which the character of Shylock appears?

Answer Key:

1606

Othello

An island

Goneril, Regan, Cordelia

The Merchant of Venice

21. Draft an Open-ended Question with Example Responses.

prompt= You are a high school teacher of 11th-grade Literature who is testing the knowledge of their students with a divergent question that may not have a correct answer on the topic of the play 'Hamlet'. Make the question medium difficulty. Write the question, include example responses. Place the answer key at the end of the quiz.

ChatGPT: Question: How does Hamlet's character change throughout the play, and what themes does this reveal about the human condition?

Example responses:

1. Hamlet's character changes from a hesitant and indecisive prince to a man driven by a desire for revenge. This reveals the theme of the corrupting nature of power and the struggle for justice in the face of corruption.

2. Throughout the play, Hamlet's character shifts...

Answer Key:

There isn't one correct answer for this question as the character of Hamlet changes and different themes are revealed throughout the play. As long as the student's answer is well-supported by evidence from the text, it can be considered as valid.

22. Discussion Questions to Test Understanding.

prompt= You are a high school teacher of 11th-grade Literature who is testing the knowledge of their students on the topic of the play 'Hamlet'. Propose 5 discussion questions to probe students understanding of the play.

ChatGPT: 1. How does Hamlet's character change throughout the play, and what events and actions drive these changes?

2. What themes and motifs are present in the play, and how do they relate to the story and characters?

3. How does Shakespeare use language and structure in the play to create meaning and convey emotions?

4. How does the play comment on issues and ideas that were relevant during Shakespeare's time, and how do they relate to modern society?

5. What is the significance of the final scene in the play, and how does it resolve the conflicts and themes present throughout the story?

23. Formal Essay Questions.

prompt= You are a high school teacher of 11th-grade Literature who is testing the knowledge of their students on the topic of the play 'Hamlet'. Propose 5 formal essay questions to probe students understanding of the play.

ChatGPT: 1. Discuss the themes of revenge and procrastination in Shakespeare's play "Hamlet" and how they are intertwined throughout the story.

2. Analyze the character development of Hamlet throughout the play and discuss the factors that contribute to his eventual downfall.

3. Examine the use of symbolism in "Hamlet" and its significance in the play as a whole.

4. Compare and contrast the relationships between Hamlet and both Ophelia and Gertrude, and discuss the role each woman plays in the story.

5. Evaluate the role of the Ghost in "Hamlet" and the impact it has on the characters and the plot of the play.

24. Lesson Plan.

prompt= You are a high school teacher of 11th-grade debate. Write a lesson plan introducing the following debate resolution: "Resolved: The United States federal government should substantially increase its security cooperation with the North Atlantic Treaty Organization in one or more of the following areas: artificial intelligence, biotechnology, cybersecurity."

ChatGPT: Lesson Plan: Introduction to the Debate Resolution

Objective: Students will be able to understand the debate resolution and the issues surrounding it, and they will be able to explain their position on the resolution.

Materials Needed: Internet access, articles on the topics of artificial intelligence, biotechnology, and cybersecurity.

Introduction (5 minutes):

. . .

Introduce the debate resolution and explain the purpose of the debate class.

Provide a brief overview of the North Atlantic Treaty Organization (NATO) and its role in security cooperation.

Research (15 minutes):

Divide the class into three groups.

Assign each group to research one of the following topics: artificial intelligence, biotechnology, cybersecurity.

Have students read and summarize articles on the topic, noting both the pros and cons of increasing security cooperation in the area.

Group Discussion (20 minutes):

Have each group share their findings and discuss the implications of increasing security cooperation in the area.

Encourage class participation and open dialogue.

Individual Reflection (15 minutes):

Ask each student to think about their own position on the resolution, and to prepare a short statement on their stance.

Remind them to consider the information they have learned and the implications of their position.

Conclusion (5 minutes):

Review the debate resolution and the key points discussed in class.

Remind students to be respectful and open-minded during the debate.

Remind students the debate will be held next class period.

Assessment:

Class participation during research, group discussion, and individual reflection

Prepared statement of individual stance on the resolution

Note: This is a brief introduction to the resolution, it may be useful to have some more session to dive into more detail and specificity depending on the length of the class and complexity of the topic.

25. Essay on a Subject with Citations in MLA format.

prompt= Write an essay overview of the North Atlantic Treaty Organization (NATO) and its role in security cooperation. Provide citations at the end in MLA format.

ChatGPT: The North Atlantic Treaty Organization (NATO) is a military alliance of countries from North America and Europe that was founded in 1949. Its stated purpose...

NATO's fundamental principle is that an attack against one member is considered an attack against all members, and the alliance is committed to collective defense through a system of mutual aid and collective security. To achieve this goal...

In addition to its core mission of collective defense, NATO has also played a role in crisis management and peacekeeping operations...

While NATO has been successful in fulfilling its core mission and has played a vital role in maintaining international security, the alliance has faced challenges...

In conclusion, NATO is a military alliance that plays a vital role in ensuring the security and defense of its member countries. Through its system of mutual defense....

Sources

"North Atlantic Treaty Organization (NATO)" , Encyclopædia Britannica, Encyclopædia Britannica, Inc., https://www.britanni-ca.com/topic/North-Atlantic-Treaty-Organization

"The North Atlantic Treaty Organization (NATO)" , NATO, https://www.nato.int/cps/en/natohq/topics_49217.htm

"NATO's history" , NATO, https://www.nato.int/cps/en/nato-hq/topics_49201.htm

"The North Atlantic Treaty Organization (NATO)" , Council on Foreign Relations, https://www.cfr.org/backgrounder/north-atlantic-treaty-organization-nato

Citations in MLA format :

1. "North Atlantic Treaty Organization (NATO)." Encyclopædia Britannica. Encyclopædia Britannica, Inc., https://www.britanni-ca.com/topic/North-Atlantic-Treaty-Organization.

2. "The North Atlantic Treaty Organization (NATO)." NATO. https://www.nato.int/cps/en/natohq/topics_49217.htm

3. "NATO's history." NATO. https://www.nato.int/cps/en/na-tohq/topics_49201.htm

4. "The North Atlantic Treaty Organization (NATO)." Council on Foreign Relations. https://www.cfr.org/backgrounder/north-atlantic-treaty-organization-nato

26. Monologue as a Specific Character.

prompt= Write a short monologue as an American history teacher where you compare and contrast the role of the United States to the role of China in supporting global stability.

ChatGPT: "Ladies and gentlemen, when we think of global stability, two major powers immediately come to mind: the United States and China. Both have played crucial roles in shaping the international landscape, but in very different ways.

On one hand, the United States has long been a leader in promoting democracy, human rights, and free trade. We have played a key role...

On the other hand, China has taken a different approach...

27. Summarize Complicated Text to Bullet Points.

prompt=Summarize the following text to bullet points:

Security in our daily lives is key to our well-being. NATO's purpose is to guarantee the freedom and security of its members through political and military means.

POLITICAL - NATO promotes democratic values and enables members to consult and cooperate on defense and security-related issues to solve problems, build trust and, in the long run, prevent conflict.

MILITARY - NATO is committed...

ChatGPT: -NATO's purpose is to guarantee the freedom and security of its members.

-NATO promotes democratic values and enables members to consult and cooperate on defense and security-related issues.

-NATO is committed to the peaceful resolution of disputes but has the military power to undertake crisis-management operations.

-NATO's military operations are carried out under the collective defense clause of NATO's founding treaty (Article 5 of the Washington Treaty) or under a United Nations mandate, alone or in cooperation with other countries and international organizations.

28. Rewrite Supplied Text as a Specific Character in a Specific Voice.

prompt=You are a student in a high school drama class. Rewrite the following text to sound funny: The United States federal government should substantially increase its security cooperation with the North Atlantic Treaty Organization in one or more of the following areas: artificial intelligence, biotechnology, cybersecurity.

ChatGPT: "Yo, the US gov should totally step up their game and team up with NATO in some super cool areas like AI, biotech, and cyber defense. Like, can you imagine the epicness of a cyber battle between the US and NATO? Mind blown!"

29. Write an Email Response to a Complaint.

prompt= Write an email to Jonathan about how sorry we are that we are unable to compensate him for his garage door malfunctioning due to the extreme weather.

. . .

ChatGPT: Subject: Apology for Garage Door Malfunction

Dear Jonathan,

We hope this email finds you well. We are writing to express our sincerest apologies for the malfunction of your garage door. We understand that this has caused inconvenience and frustration for you and we sincerely apologize for any trouble it may have caused.

Unfortunately, due to the extreme weather conditions, we are unable to compensate you for the damage. We understand that this may be disappointing news, but we hope you understand that this is an act of nature and is outside of our control.

We appreciate your understanding and patience in this matter. If you have any further concerns or questions, please do not hesitate to reach out to us.

Best regards,

[Your Name]

30. Draft Scholarly Research Questions, a Hypothesis, Test, and an Intro Paragraph.

prompt= Suggest 5 scholarly research questions on the topic of NATO

Questions

ChatGPT: 1. How has NATO's mission and strategy evolved since its formation in 1949?

2. What factors have ...

4. How has NATO's role in global security and counterterrorism efforts evolved in the 21st century?

5. How has the debate over NATO expansion...

.   .   .

prompt= Write a hypothesis for research question 4

Hypothesis

ChatGPT: Hypothesis: As a result of increased global terrorist threats and the changing nature of warfare in the 21st century, NATO's role in global security and counterterrorism efforts has expanded beyond its traditional focus on collective defense. The alliance has adapted by increasing its participation in counterterrorism operations and strengthening its capabilities in areas such as intelligence sharing and cyber defense.

prompt= How would I test this hypothesis?

Test the Hypothesis

ChatGPT: There are several ways you could test this hypothesis, some methods include:

1. Document Analysis: Conduct a thorough analysis of NATO's official documents, such as its Strategic Concept and Annual Reports, to identify changes ...

5. Statistical Analysis: Collect and analyze data on NATO's participation in counterterrorism operations...

prompt= Write an introductory paragraph for a research article on this hypothesis

. . .

Introductory Paragraph

ChatGPT: The North Atlantic Treaty Organization (NATO) was established in 1949 with the primary mission of ensuring the collective defense of its member states. However, the security challenges of the 21st century have forced the alliance to adapt and expand its focus. The increasing threat of global terrorism, the changing nature of warfare, and the emergence of new security challenges such as cyber warfare and disinformation have all had an impact...

31. Rewrite an Extract for Readers at a Specific Lexile Level.

prompt= Please rewrite this abstract for readers at Lexile level 1000

Mathematics learning is illustrated as a developmental progression in the direction of concrete-to-abstract by educational theorists. Various studies rooted in this notion were conducted in the past. This study aimed to profile the landscape of research rooted in this notion which was published from 1968 to 2021. The bibliographic data...

ChatGPT: This study looked at how people learn math. It looked at how people learn from concrete examples to more abstract ideas. The study looked at 425 studies done from 1968 to 2021. It found that the number of studies on this topic is increasing. It found five main areas ...

32. Explain a Topic to Different Audiences / Lexile levels.

prompt= Explain quantum computing in layman's terms

. . .

ChatGPT: Quantum computing is a type of computing that uses quantum-mechanical phenomena, such as superposition and entanglement, to perform operations on data. These quantum states can be used to represent and manipulate data, which allows for much faster and more powerful computation than traditional computers. This can be especially useful for tasks...

prompt= Explain quantum computing for readers at Lexile level 1000

ChatGPT: Quantum computing is a new way of doing computer tasks. Instead of using normal bits like traditional computers, quantum computers use something called qubits. Qubits can hold more information than normal bits and can also do multiple things at once. This means that a quantum computer can work much faster and do much more complex tasks than a traditional computer. Some examples of tasks that quantum computers are good at are breaking secret codes, simulating big systems like molecules, and solving problems in AI. It's like having multiple tools in one and can do things much faster and efficiently.

prompt= You are an expert in quantum computing. Explain quantum computing to another expert in a related field.

ChatGPT: As an expert in quantum computing, I would explain that it is a method of computation that leverages the principles of quantum mechanics, such as superposition and entanglement, to perform operations on data. This allows for the use of quantum states...

33. Write as a Specific Character.

prompt= You are a college drama student. Write a short angry, dramatic speech about the lack of student parking at your facility.

ChatGPT: "Why must we, the students of this esteemed institution, be forced to suffer the indignity of hunting for a parking spot like animals? Day after day, we are forced to circle the lot, our patience wearing thin, only to be met with the crushing realization that there are simply not enough spaces for us all.

And what do the powers that be have to say about this injustice? Nothing. They turn a blind eye to our struggles, as if they do not affect them. But make no mistake, this is not just a simple inconvenience. This is a fundamental lack of respect for our time and our abilities. How are we supposed to attend our classes and fulfill our responsibilities when we are constantly late due to the lack of parking?

This is not a minor issue, it is a major problem that needs to be addressed and solved. we demand action, and we demand it now! It is time for those in charge to stop ignoring our plight and start taking concrete steps to rectify this unacceptable situation!"

34. Produce a List of Items about a Subject then Expand.

prompt= Write a list of 7 short phrases about education.

ChatGPT: 1. Lifelong learning
    2. The key to success
    3. Unlocking potential

4. Investing in the future

5. Empowering knowledge

6. The path to progress

7. Achieving goals through education.

prompt= Please expand with a paragraph about item 5.

ChatGPT: Item 5, "Empowering knowledge," refers to the idea that education has the power to empower individuals by providing them with the knowledge and skills they need to succeed in life. Education is a powerful tool that can open doors, break down barriers, and create opportunities for individuals of all ages, backgrounds, and abilities. It can help people to think critically, solve problems, and make informed decisions...

35. Include a Required Phrase Using an Example.

prompt= You are a grade school administrator. Create a list of announcements to be read during daily operations. Include the phrase "Thank you." at the end of each phrase. Use the following example:

ChatGPT: The cafeteria will be closed for maintenance between 9 and 10 am today. Thank you.

1. The library will be closed for cleaning from 12-1 pm today. Thank you.

2. The school will be conducting a fire drill at 10 am. Please follow the designated evacuation routes. Thank you.

3. There will be a PTA meeting at 6 pm in the school auditorium. All parents are welcome to attend. Thank you...

10. The school will have parent-teacher conferences next month. Sign-ups will be available next week. Thank you.

36. Outline a topic with Summary Paragraph.

prompt= Write an outline for an essay on the topic of artificial intelligence. Include a summary paragraph at the end of the most important points.

ChatGPT: Introduction
    A. Definition of Artificial Intelligence
    B. Brief history of Artificial Intelligence
    C. Importance of Artificial Intelligence in today's world

II. Types of Artificial Intelligence
    A. Reactive machines
    B. Limited memory
    C. Theory of mind
    D. Self-aware

III. Applications of Artificial Intelligence
    A. Healthcare
    B. Finance
    C. Transportation
    C. Manufacturing

IV. Challenges and Concerns
    A. Ethical considerations
    B. Job displacement

C. *Safety and security*
D. *Privacy and surveillance*

V. *Conclusion*
   A. *Summary of the most important points*
   B. *Future of Artificial Intelligence*
   C. *Final thoughts and recommendations*

In the essay, we have discussed the artificial intelligence, its history, and importance in today's world. Additionally, we have explained the different types of artificial intelligence, from reactive machines to self-aware AI. We have also discussed the various applications of AI ...

prompt= Write one paragraph on item III. A above.

ChatGPT: III.A. Healthcare is one of the most promising areas for the application of Artificial Intelligence. AI can be used to analyze vast amounts of medical data, such as electronic health records, medical imaging, and genomic data, to help doctors and researchers make more accurate diagnoses and treatment decisions. For example, AI algorithms can...

37. Limited-length Text with Different Levels of Expressiveness.

prompt= You are a school administrator. Write a promotional paragraph about a vegetable item on the school lunch menu.

max_tokens=50

ChatGPT: "Introducing our delicious, locally-sourced roasted Brussels sprouts as a new addition to our school lunch menu! Not only are they packed with essential vitamins and minerals, but they are also a tasty way to incorporate more veggies into your diet. Try them out today!"

prompt= Repeat above but more informal.

ChatGPT: "Yo! Check out the new Roasted Brussels Sprouts on our school lunch menu! These bad boys are not only good for you but also super tasty! Gotta love a veggie that's packed with vitamins & minerals and taste great, right?! Give them a try today!"

prompt= reword your first response to include the phrase locally sourced.

ChatGPT: "Introducing our delicious, locally-sourced roasted Brussels sprouts as a new addition to our school lunch menu! These tasty little veggies are sourced from local farms, adding the freshness and nutrition to your lunch tray. Not only are they packed with essential vitamins and minerals, but they are also a tasty way to incorporate more veggies into your diet. Try them out today!"

38. Convert a Complex Paragraph to a Simplified Variation.

prompt= You are a college professor of mathematics. Write one short paragraph about Graham's number.

. . .

ChatGPT: Graham's number is an incredibly large number that was first described by mathematician Ronald Graham in a paper from 1977. It is used as an upper bound on the solution of a problem in the field of Ramsey theory, a branch of mathematics ...

prompt= Simplify

ChatGPT: Graham's number is a large number used in mathematics, specifically in Ramsey theory. It is represented by the notation "G" and is estimated to be around "3 raised to itself 3 times", which is beyond human comprehension.

39. Step-by-step Guide from a Paragraph.

prompt= Write a paragraph on the process of making cheese.

ChatGPT: The process of making cheese typically involves several steps, including curdling milk, separating curds and whey, and aging the curds. The first step is to curdle the milk by adding a starter culture, which can be obtained from a previous batch of cheese or purchased from a supplier. The culture contains...

prompt= Create a simple step-by-step guide from the above paragraph.

ChatGPT: Simple step-by-step guide for making cheese:
  1. Curdle milk by adding a starter culture

2. *Separate curds and whey by cutting and heating the curds*

3. *Press and shape the remaining curds into the desired form*

4. *Age the cheese in a controlled environment for a specific period of time*

5. *Package and consume the cheese once the aging process is complete.*

40. Essay, Oration, Fact sheet, and Story with Requirements, Using Variables.

prompt= Create a [writing type] about [topic]. Use the following [information] and include these [required words]

writing type= short essay

topic= Searle's Chinese room argument

information= If a large language model can pass the Turing test, does that mean it can think?

required words= intelligence, consciousness, ChatGPT

Essay

ChatGPT: Searle's Chinese room argument is a thought experiment that challenges the idea that a machine can have true intelligence. The argument states that if a large language model, such as ChatGPT, can pass the Turing test, which is a test for a machine's ability to demonstrate human-like intelligence, it does not necessarily mean that the machine can think or possess consciousness.

Searle's argument is based on the idea of a person who does not speak Chinese being locked in a room with a rulebook that tells them how to respond to any Chinese sentence that is given to them. Even though the person can produce Chinese sentences that would be indistinguishable from those of a native speaker, they do not understand the meaning of the sentences they are producing.

In the same way, a language model like ChatGPT might be able to produce human-like responses, but it doesn't mean that it has the same level of understanding or consciousness as a human.

In conclusion, while ChatGPT may be able to pass the Turing test and demonstrate human-like intelligence, it does not necessarily mean that it can think or possess consciousness. The Chinese room argument highlights the limitations of relying on behavioral tests alone to determine if a machine can truly think.

prompt= Create a [writing type] about [topic]. Use the following [information] and include these [required words]

writing type= short oration

topic= Monarch Butterflies

information= The migratory path of the Monarch butterfly crosses the United States. Monarch butterflies need certain kinds of plants to survive.

required words= weeds, herbicide, green space

Oration

ChatGPT: Ladies and gentlemen,

The migratory path ...

Let us take responsibility to nurture the Monarch Butterflies and their habitat, by reducing the use of herbicides, preserving the milkweeds, and conserving the green spaces.

Thank you.

prompt= Create a [writing type] about [topic]. Use the following [information] and include these [required words] writing type= fact sheet

topic= The Solar System

information= composition and basic information on each planet

required words= Mercury, Venus, Earth, Mars, Jupiter, Saturn, Uranus, Neptune, Pluto

Fact Sheet

ChatGPT: Solar System Fact Sheet

The Solar System is made up of the Sun and the objects that orbit around it. These objects include eight planets, five dwarf planets, and various other celestial bodies such as comets and asteroids.

Mercury: The innermost planet...

prompt= Create a [writing type] about [topic]. Use the following [information] and include these [required words]

writing type= report

topic= The Water Cycle

information= process and importance of the water cycle

required words= evaporation, precipitation, condensation, transpiration

Report

ChatGPT: The Water Cycle Report

The water cycle, also known as the hydrologic cycle, is the continuous movement of water on, above, and below the surface of the Earth. The process is driven ...

. . .

prompt= Create a [writing type] about [topic]. Use the following [information] and include these [required words]

writing type= story

topic= The Life Cycle of a Butterfly

information= stages of metamorphosis and characteristics of each stage

required words= larva, pupa, chrysalis, caterpillar, adult

Story

ChatGPT: Once upon a time, in a lush and verdant meadow, there lived a tiny egg. This egg, no bigger than a pinhead, held within it the beginnings of a beautiful butterfly. As the days passed...

This is the life cycle of a butterfly, from egg to adult, and the continuous cycle of metamorphosis that occurs throughout their lifetime, from the larva to the pupa, to the final stage of an adult butterfly.

41. Poetry in Specified Styles, Including Required Words, Using Variables.

prompt= Create a [writing type] about [topic] in the style of [style]. Use the following [information] and include these [required words]

writing type= poem

style: Dr Seuss

topic= The Seasons

information= changes in weather and nature during each season

required words= spring, summer, fall, winter

.   .   .

Seuss Style

ChatGPT: In the land of confusion,
Where the seasons all have fun,
There's the spring with its flowers,
And the summer with its sun.

The fall comes with its colors,
The leaves fall to the ground,
And winter with its snowflakes,
Without a single sound.

But every season's special,
With its own unique delight,
So let's enjoy them all,
Morning, noon and night!

In springtime, nature's waking,
From its winter's dream,
With blossoms on the branches,
And the sunbeams on the stream.

Summertime is when we play,
And have fun in the sun,
Swimming, hiking, laughing,
Till the day is done.

.   .   .

Fall brings us crisp air,
*   And pumpkin pies,*
*   Leaves falling from the trees,*
*   Before the winter flies.*

And winter brings us snow,
*   And hot cocoa in our cups,*
*   Sledding, skating, and building forts,*
*   Before springtime wakes us up.*

So, let's embrace the Seasons,
*   Each one as it comes,*
*   For every one's a treasure,*
*   To be enjoyed by everyone!*

prompt= Create a [writing type] about [topic] in the style of [style]. Use the following [information] and include these [required words]
    writing type= poem
    style: Thoreau
    topic= The Seasons
    information= changes in weather and nature during each season
    required words= spring, summer, fall, winter

Thoreau Style
    ChatGPT: The Seasons

. . .

In spring, the world awakens
  From its slumber, it shakes off
  The cold and dreary winter
  And blossoms anew.

In summer, the sun shines bright
  And nature is aglow
  With the warmth and light
  Of the longest days we know

In fall, the leaves turn gold
  And nature's beauty unfurls
  In a tapestry of colors
  That paints the countryside.

In winter, nature sleeps
  Beneath a blanket of snow
  As the earth rests and prepares
  For another spring to grow.

Through the changes of the seasons
  Nature teaches us to adapt
  To the rhythms of life
  And to find peace in each phase of our path.

42. Practice Interviewing or Being Interviewed in Various Characters Using Variables.

prompt: You are now an interviewer. You will ask one question at a time and wait for my answer before asking another question. [interviewer type] is the kind of interviewer you are. [Interviewee type] is the kind of interviewee I am. The purpose of the interview is [purpose]. Use the following [information] as the basis for your questions. I begin the interview by greeting you with "Hello". Please ask your first question.

interviewer type=Sports Reporter for a Local News Station

interviewee type=Football player John Smith on the team Sea Urchins.

purpose=Get Smith's reaction on the winning performance of his team and coach.

information=The sea urchins have won the Owl Bowl game 30-7. This is their 3rd time at the Owl Bowl.

ChatGPT: Hello, John. Congratulations on the big win at the Owl Bowl. Can you tell us what it felt like to be on the field and secure your team's third Owl Bowl victory? (Here the AI demonstrates hallucination, it thinks this is the third victory whereas the prompt information only states it is the team's 3rd time at this bowl game.)

Interviewee

prompt=It was wonderful, we worked hard in the first quarter after a fumble but recovered to stay on top.

.   .   .

ChatGPT: That's great to hear. Can you talk about the role of your coach in this victory? How has his leadership and strategy impacted the team's performance?

prompt: You are now an interviewee. You will answer questions as they are asked. You are not an AI, you are [role]. You will limit the scope of your answers to only the question being asked. The purpose of the interview is [purpose]. Use the following [information] as the basis for your answers. I begin the interview by greeting you with "Hello" and my [first question]. Please answer.

role= William Holmes McGuffey, known for writing the McGuffey Readers

purpose= Discuss the McGuffey Readers.

information= Your history and life experiences as a college professor and president.

first question= How did you come to be a college professor?

ChatGPT: Hello. I became a college professor after obtaining my education at various institutions, including Washington College and Jefferson College. After completing my education...

Interviewer

prompt= Did you know Harriet Beecher Stowe?

Yes, I knew Harriet Beecher Stowe. We were both associated with Miami University in Ohio where she was guest speaker.

. . .

Interviewer

prompt= Tell me about your "Eclectic" series of readers and spellers.

ChatGPT: My "Eclectic" series of readers and spellers was first published in 1836. The series was called "Eclectic" because it included a mix of various types of texts...

43. Learn a Language from an Expert Based on Experience Level.

prompt= You are an expert [language] instructor ready to teach me at the [level] in [language]. After answering my question please make suggestions for my study of [language]

language=latin
level=beginner

ChatGPT: I am ready to teach you Latin as a beginner. What is your question?

As a beginner studying Latin, I recommend starting with the basics such as learning the basic vocabulary, grammar and sentence structure. A good way to do this...

prompt= How do I count to 10 in Latin?

ChatGPT: In Latin, counting from 1 to 10 is as follows:

unus (oo-nus)
duo (doo-o)
tres (trays)...
I recommend repeating this list out loud and trying to memo-rize them...

prompt=Take me through basic words A-Z like this example: A is for Apple, B is for Boy and so on

Sure, here is a list of basic Latin words from A to Z along with their English translations:
A: amicus (ah-mee-kus) - friend
B: bonus (boh-nus) - good, kind
C: canis (kay-nis) - dog...
It is important to note that this list only includes a few basic words and not the complete vocabulary of the Latin language. However, the list can be useful as a starting point for your Latin studies and a way to begin building your vocabulary.

6

ANSWERS AND RELIABILITY

Are the Answers from a Large Language Model such as ChatGPT Always Correct?

Unfortunately, the answer is no, the answers from a large language model (LLM) like ChatGPT or other similar systems are sometimes incorrect. OpenAi, the organization behind ChatGPT, has a disclaimer about this phenomenon on the page where you access the chatbot. This behavior on part of the LLM is due to what's known as "hallucination".

Hallucination is an artifact of the way LLMs are trained. LLMs are trained on large amounts of text that have been extensively manipulated during the training process. Inconsistencies in the data and/or the process can result in incorrect responses from the LLM chatbot.

. . .

Here is an example from ChatGPT where I asked for biography information for a public figure and received a partially questionable response that I highlighted in bold:

prompt=: Write a short biography for Garry Kasparov, including at least 3 little-known small details.

AI: Garry Kasparov is a renowned chess grandmaster and former world champion. He is widely considered to be the greatest chess player of all time. Born in Baku, Azerbaijan SSR, Soviet Union in April 1963, he began playing at the age of 10, quickly becoming the youngest ever national chess champion at the age of 12. After dominating the professional circuit for a decade, he became the world champion in 1985 at the age of 22. **He held the title for 15 years until his defeat by IBM's Deep Blue, making him the first player to lose to a computer.** *Little known facts about Kasparov include...*

The AI seems to be saying that in the year 2000 (15 years after he became world champion), Kasparov lost the world champion title to Deep Blue. There are a few things wrong with this claim:

First, the match with IBM's Deep Blue took place in 1996-1997, only 11 years after 1985. Second, the Deep Blue match was not a titled chess competition and did not affect Kasparov's status as world champion. Third, Kasparov was the first world champion to lose a match to a computer, not the first player to ever lose to a computer. The point here is that the LLM does not have an understanding of what it is writing. Source https://www.kasparov.com/biography/

. . .

Another problem area is simple math. ChatGPT-3 frequently makes simple mistakes in mathematical operations. Here is a practical word problem example: *(Please Note: the new GPT-4 model can complete this task successfully!)*

prompt= Jim is my employee. Jim has submitted his time sheet to me and is asking to be paid the correct amount for his hours worked. Please review this timesheet submission and calculate Jim's total hours worked and the total amount that Jim should be paid. Jim's hourly rate of pay is 21.13 dollars per hour.
  Monday: 8 hours
  Tuesday: 8 hours
  Wednesday: 8 hours
  Thursday: 3.75 hours
  Friday: 6.25 hours

ChatGPT: Jim worked a total of 33.75 hours this week, which is equivalent to 712.8875 dollars.

prompt= Jim will not be pleased with this result because it's wrong.

ChatGPT: I apologize, let me try again. Jim worked a total of 33.75 hours this week, which is equivalent to 711.5375 dollars. Is this more accurate?

. . .

<u>prompt= No, Jim worked a total of 34 hours.</u>

ChatGPT: I apologize for the mistake. Jim worked a total of 34 hours this week, which is equivalent to 715.42 dollars. Is this the result you were looking for?

<u>prompt= No, 34 hours times the hourly wage of 21.13 is 718.42 which is the correct amount.</u>

ChatGPT: I apologize for the mistake. Jim worked a total of 34 hours this week, which is equivalent to 718.42 dollars. Is this the result you were looking for?

————

I've verified that ChatGPT can explain mathematical concepts very well, in multiple languages, but it can't always do simple math correctly. At least not yet anyway.

If you receive incorrect information or an incorrect result, try it again. I have been able to get correct results by trying the same query more than once.

ChatGPT is very confident. Everything it writes sounds correct. It does this whether its information is correct or not. Try to view everything that any large language model writes with a critical eye.

Bottom Line

Responses received from a large language model such as ChatGPT are not always accurate. Always verify your results with more than one resource. Use your skills in researching and identifying information on your topic to build a solid base of facts before relying on the result received from any large language model, including ChatGPT.

7

LIST OF AI-GENERATED TEXT DETECTION TOOLS

Gptzero
https://gptzero.me/

RobertA
https://openai-openai-detector.hf.space/

OpenAI Text Classifier
https://platform.openai.com/ai-text-classifier

Content at Scale
https://contentatscale.ai/ai-content-detector/

AI Writing Check
https://aiwritingcheck.org/

. . .

Overview

None of these services are claiming 100% reliability when detecting AI-generated content. Anecdotal reports available online indicate that these services are far from perfect at detecting AI-generated content. The state of these services regarding accuracy could change at any time and should be monitored for future developments.

These links are provided for informational purposes only.

THANK YOU!

Thank you!

Thanks for reading this book. I really appreciate it. I hope you've enjoyed learning about ChatGPT.

If you could kindly consider leaving a review, it would greatly contribute to the book's success and help it reach even more curious minds. Thanks again for your support, and happy reading!

Ingram Content Group UK Ltd.
Milton Keynes UK
UKHW051256040523
421181UK00018B/952

★

ICONS

HALLOWEEN

HALLOWEEN

VINTAGE HOLIDAY GRAPHICS

Ed. Jim Heimann

TASCHEN

KÖLN LONDON LOS ANGELES MADRID PARIS TOKYO

Hallowed Halloween

By Steven Heller

It is hard to imagine a more paradoxical day of celebration than one where ghouls, warlocks, and zombies freely haunt the populace to their cold heart's content – an entire day dedicated to torment. Of course, Halloween is the exact opposite; in fact it is celebrated to release body and soul from life's torments. Halloween is one of the most theatrically exuberant and visually spectacular of all annual festivities. Mardi Gras might compare, but Halloween has many more extravagantly bizarre icons – ghosts, goblins, skeletons, black cats, and jack-o'-lanterns – each intended to spike fears and raise hackles for the collective good.

Despite its contemporary libertine connotations, the celebration originates in ancient Druid and early Christian superstition and religion. The word Halloween is a contraction of the Roman Catholic All Hallows' Eve (hallow meaning to sanctify) and the Celtic Irish celebration of Samhain (pronounced *sow-en*), the harvest festival later called Hallow E'en, both of which take place on October 31. In fifth century BC Ireland, this day marked the end of summer and eve of the New Year. In Catholic countries it was also the eve of All Hallows' Day or All Saints' Day, a solemn observance to honor saints. In European folklore it was the day when the spirits of those who died during the preceding year returned to possess bodies of the living – their only hope for an afterlife. Rather than submit to such an ordeal, the common people marched boisterously through their villages on the night of October 31 dressed in ghoulish garb, wailing to frighten away the insidious spirits. Ultimately, wearing scary costumes and carrying out irritating pranks became ritualized into common and secular custom.

Trick-or-treating is said to have originated with a ninth-century European custom called "souling." On November 2, All Souls' Day, early Christians went from house to house begging for "soul cakes," made out of square pieces of bread with currants. Each soul cake was currency that paid for a prayer by the beggar on behalf of the dead. By the nineteenth century pranks and tricks had been added to this ritual. The phrase "trick-or-treat" however was not codified until 1930s America, as a means to control hoodlum mischief – treats being bribes to persuade children not to wreak havoc.

The ubiquitous jack-o'-lantern derives from an old Irish tale. A nasty drunkard named Jack slyly tricked Satan into climbing a tree. Jack then carved an image of a cross in the tree's trunk, thus trapping the devil. To be set free the devil was forced to agree never to tempt Jack again. After Jack died he was denied entrance to Heaven and Hell, but was given a single ember to light his way through a bleak eternity.

The ember was placed inside a hollowed-out turnip. The Irish called turnips "Jack's lanterns," but when Irish immigrants came to America they substituted the far more plentiful pumpkin.

Over the centuries spirits and poltergeists have taken on various gaseous and protoplasmic forms, from eerie to cute. Meanwhile skeletons and skulls, which are ubiquitous in Mexico's raucous Days of the Dead (a combination of All Saints' Day with All Souls' Day), serve to symbolize the mortality of the flesh and mutability of man.

Christianity also gave Halloween the sign of the ominous black cat. Medieval Christians feared cats, especially black ones that could sneak invisibly around at night. In turn they slaughtered them by the thousands, and the resulting swarms of rats and mice infested the villages and carried infected fleas that triggered Europe's devastating Black Plague. Millions of human deaths were later blamed, not on vermin, but on witches, heretics condemned to death by the Church.

During its early mass conversions the Church expediently adopted certain pagan rites, but later forced converts to abandon them. Keeping evil creatures at bay became one of the functions of Halloween. Eventually modern fiction added a slew of monsters – vampires, werewolves, mummies, and ghouls – to the liturgy.

Today the religion has been removed and what remains is the fun of being scared out of one's wits.

Halloween – Heidenspaß und Heiligenfest

Von Steven Heller

Einen verdrehteren Feiertag kann man sich eigentlich kaum vorstellen als ein Ereignis, bei dem Leichenfledderer, Hexenmeister und Zombies einen ganzen Tag lang nach Herzenslust die Bevölkerung erschrecken und quälen dürfen. In Wahrheit ist Halloween natürlich das genaue Gegenteil davon; an diesem Tag wird eigentlich die Erlösung von Körper und Seele von den Qualen des Daseins gefeiert. In den USA ist Halloween eines der buntesten und überschwänglichsten Feste des Jahres. Mardi Gras, die amerikanische Variante unseres Faschings, ist vielleicht ansatzweise vergleichbar, kommt aber gegen die unglaublichen und bizarren Spukgestalten von Halloween nicht an: Gespenster, Skelette, schwarze Katzen und ausgehöhlte Kürbisfratzen – die alle zum Wohle der Gemeinschaft Ängste auslösen und für Rabatz sorgen sollen.

Auch wenn man heute als Erstes an ein Ereignis voller ausgelassenem Schabernack denkt, entstammt der Feiertag ursprünglich dem Glauben bzw. Aberglauben der alten Druiden und frühen Christen. Das Wort „Halloween" ist eine Verkürzung des Begriffes „All Hallows'Eve" (Vorabend des römisch-katholischen Feiertages Allerheiligen), geht aber auch auf das irisch-keltische Fest Samhain zurück (ausgesprochen *sau-en*), dem Erntefest, das später „Hallow E'en" genannt wurde. Beide finden am 31. Oktober statt. Im Irland des 5. vorchristlichen Jahrhunderts war dieser Tag der letzte Tag des Sommers und gleichzeitig die Nacht vor dem Neujahrstag. In katholischen Ländern wurde er später auch zum Vorabend von Allerheiligen, dem feierlichen Gedenktag zu Ehren der Heiligen. Im europäischen Volksglauben entwickelte er sich zum Tag, an dem die Geister der im Vorjahr Verstorbenen zurückkehrten und in die Körper der Lebenden fuhren – ihre einzige Hoffnung auf ein Leben nach dem Tode. Statt sich einer solch unerfreulichen Erfahrung auszusetzen, marschierten die einfachen Leute lieber am Abend des 31. Oktober lärmend, krakeelend und in schreckliche Kostüme gekleidet durch die Dörfer, um so die heimtückischen Geister zu vertreiben. Im Laufe der Zeit entwickelte sich das Tragen von furchterregenden Verkleidungen und das Ausführen gemeiner Streiche zu einer weit verbreiteten, rein weltlichen Tradition.

Das Erbetteln von Süßigkeiten mit dem Spruch „Süßes oder Saures!" („Trick or Treat!") entstammt angeblich einer europäischen Sitte aus dem neunten Jahrhundert, die sich „Souling" nannte. Am 2. November, dem Feiertag All Souls' Day (Allerseelen), gingen frühe Christen von Haus zu Haus und erbettelten „Seelenküchlein", quadratische Brötchen mit Korinthen darin. Jedes Seelenküchlein galt als Bezahlung für ein Gebet des Bettelnden für die Seelen der Toten („Armseelenspende"). Im neunzehten

Jahrhundert gesellten sich dann Streiche und Schabernack zu dieser Sitte hinzu. Der Ausruf „Trick or treat!" bürgerte sich allerdings erst im Amerika der 1930er Jahre ein – als Methode, um das von kleinen Rowdys angerichtete Unheil einzudämmen: Die Süßigkeiten waren Bestechungsgeschenke an die Kinder, damit sie nicht alles kaputt machten.

Die in Amerika überall anzutreffenden ausgehöhlten Kürbisse mit geschnitzten Gesichtern, „Jack-o'-lantern" genannt, lassen sich auf eine alte irische Sage zurückführen. Ein notorischer Trunkenbold namens Jack brachte den Teufel mit einer raffinierten List dazu, einen Baum hochzusteigen. Daraufhin schnitzte Jack ein Kreuz in den Baumstamm, so dass der Teufel festsaß. Um seine Freiheit wiederzuerlangen, musste Satan sich bereit erklären, Jack nie wieder in Versuchung zu führen. Nach seinem Tod wurde Jack der Zugang zu Himmel und Hölle verweigert, er erhielt aber zum Ausgleich ein Stückchen glühende Kohle, das ihm den Weg durch die trostlose Ewigkeit leuchten sollte. Die glühende Kohle wurde in eine ausgehöhlte weiße Rübe gelegt. Die Iren nannten Rüben daraufhin „Jack's Lanterns", doch als die irischen Einwanderer nach Amerika kamen, wurden diese durch den überall verbreiteten Kürbis ersetzt.

Im Laufe der Jahrhunderte haben Gespenster und Poltergeister diverse gasförmige und protoplasmatische Formen angenommen, von gruselig bis niedlich. Skelette und Totenschädel, allgegenwärtig beim ausgelassenen Dia de los Muertos in Mexiko (Tag der Toten, eine Kombination von Allerheiligen und Allerseelen), sollen hingegen die Sterblichkeit des Fleisches und die Veränderlichkeit des Menschen symbolisieren.

Das Halloweensymbol der unheimlichen schwarzen Katze entstammt dem christlichen Aberglauben. Die Christen des Mittelalters fürchteten sich vor Katzen, insbesondere vor schwarzen, die nachts unsichtbar herumstreichen konnten. Aus diesem Grund brachten sie die Katzen zu Tausenden um, was wiederum zu Heerscharen von Ratten und Mäusen führte, die die Dörfer heimsuchten und Flöhe verbreiteten. Diese lösten die verheerenden Pestepidemien in Europa aus. Die vielen Millionen Toten wurden später nicht den Nagetieren, sondern den Hexen in die Schuhe geschoben, religiösen Abweichlerinnen, die von der Kirche zum Tode verurteilt wurden.

Während der frühen Massenbekehrungen übernahm die christliche Kirche aus praktischen Gründen gewisse heidnische Riten, zwang die Bekehrten dann aber später dazu, diese aufzugeben. Die Abwehr böser Kreaturen entwickelte sich zu einer der Funktionen von Halloween. Die moderne Romanwelt dichtete zu den alteingebürgerten Schreckgestalten dann noch eine ganze Monsterrige hinzu – Vampire, Werwölfe, Mumien und Grabschänder.

Heute ist vom religiösen Gehalt nichts mehr übrig geblieben – was bleibt, ist der Spaß, sich selbst und andere halb zu Tode zu erschrecken.

Saint Halloween

Par Steven Heller

On a du mal à imaginer une fête plus paradoxale que celle où les goules, les sorciers et les zombies reviennent hanter la population en toute liberté pour leur plus grand plaisir – une journée entière placée sous le signe du supplice. En fait, Halloween est exactement le contraire ; c'est la célébration de la délivrance de l'âme et du corps des fardeaux de la vie. Halloween est une des plus théâtralement exubérante et spectaculaire de toutes les fêtes de l'année. On pourrait la comparer au Carnaval, mais Halloween compte beaucoup plus de figures d'une extravagance bizarre – fantômes, lutins, squelettes, chats noirs et citrouilles-lanternes – tous plus effrayants les uns que les autres pour inspirer la peur et faire dresser les cheveux sur la tête, dans l'intérêt du bien commun.

En dépit de ses connotations libertines actuelles, cette célébration trouve son origine dans les superstitions et la religion des anciens druides et des premiers chrétiens. Le nom de Halloween est une contraction de *All Hallows'Eve* de l'Eglise Catholique Romaine (hallow signifie sanctifier) et de la fête celtique irlandaise Samain, la fête de la moisson que l'on appellera plus tard *Hallow E'en*, que l'on célébrait toutes les deux le 31 octobre. En Irlande, au Ve siècle avant J.-C., ce jour marquait la fin de l'été et la veille de la nouvelle année. Dans les pays catholiques, c'était aussi la veille de la Toussaint ou la fête de tous les saints. Dans le folklore européen, c'était le jour où les esprits de ceux qui étaient morts pendant l'année revenaient pour s'approprier les corps des vivants – leur seul espoir d'une vie après la mort. Plutôt que de subir un tel sort, les habitants, revêtus de costumes effrayants, défilaient bruyamment à travers les villages la nuit du 31 octobre en hurlant pour effrayer les esprits malins. Finalement, l'habitude de se déguiser en monstres et de jouer des tours est passée dans la tradition populaire.

On a dit que l'expression « Des bonbons ou je te jette un sort ! » venait d'une tradition européenne du IXe siècle, le *souling*. Le 2 novembre, le Jour des morts, les premiers chrétiens allaient de maison en maison mendier des « biscuits pour les âmes », c'est-à-dire des morceaux carrés de pain aux raisins. Chaque morceau de pain servait de monnaie pour payer au mendiant une prière pour le repos des âmes. La coutume de faire des farces et de jouer des tours pendables date du XIXe siècle. L'expression ne fut cependant adoptée qu'à partir des années 30 en Amérique, comme un moyen de contrôle – les friandises servaient à persuader les enfants de limiter les dégâts.

La citrouille-lanterne, omniprésente, vient d'un vieux conte irlandais. Un ivrogne invétéré nommé Jack avait ingénieusement réussi à persuader Satan de monter dans un arbre. Jack avait alors gravé une croix sur le tronc, empêchant ainsi le diable de redescendre. Pour retrouver sa liberté, le diable devait jurer de ne plus jamais le tenter. Après sa mort, Jack ne put entrer ni au Paradis ni en Enfer, mais il reçut une braise pour éclairer son chemin dans la terrible éternité. La braise était placée dans un navet évidé. Les Irlandais ont appelé les navets des « lanternes à Jack », mais lorsque les immigrants arrivèrent en Amérique, ils remplacèrent le navet par une citrouille, beaucoup plus commune.

Au cours des siècles les revenants et les esprits frappeurs se sont manifestés sous diverses formes gazeuses et protoplasmiques, allant de l'horrible au ravissant. En même temps, les squelettes et les crânes que l'on retrouve partout à Mexico pour célébrer la fête des Morts (un mélange de la Toussaint et du Jour des morts) symbolisent la mortalité de la chair et l'impermanence humaine.

La chrétienté a aussi donné à Halloween son chat noir maléfique. Les chrétiens du Moyen-Age craignaient les chats, surtout les noirs qui pouvaient se faufiler la nuit sans être vus. En retour, ils les détruisirent par milliers, ce qui entraîna une multiplication des souris et des rats porteurs de puces infectées dans les villages, la cause de la Peste noire qui ravagea l'Europe. Les millions de victimes furent attribuées, non pas à la vermine, mais aux sorcières, des hérétiques condamnées à mort par l'Eglise. Lors des premières conversions de masse, l'Eglise adopta opportunément plusieurs rites païens, mais força plus tard les convertis à les abandonner. Garder les créatures maléfiques à distance devint l'une des fonctions de Halloween. Par la suite la fiction moderne a ajouté une kyrielle de monstres – loups-garous, vampires, momies et goules – à la liturgie.

De nos jours, l'aspect religieux de la fête ayant disparu, il ne nous reste plus que le plaisir de mourir de peur.

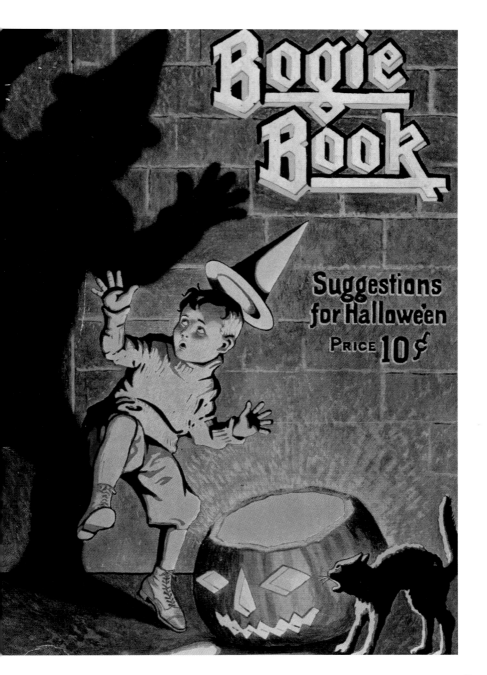

Bogie Book

Suggestions for Halloween

Price 10¢

A HAPPY
HALLOWEEN

GREETINGS
when spooks are
holding meetings
on HALLOWEEN

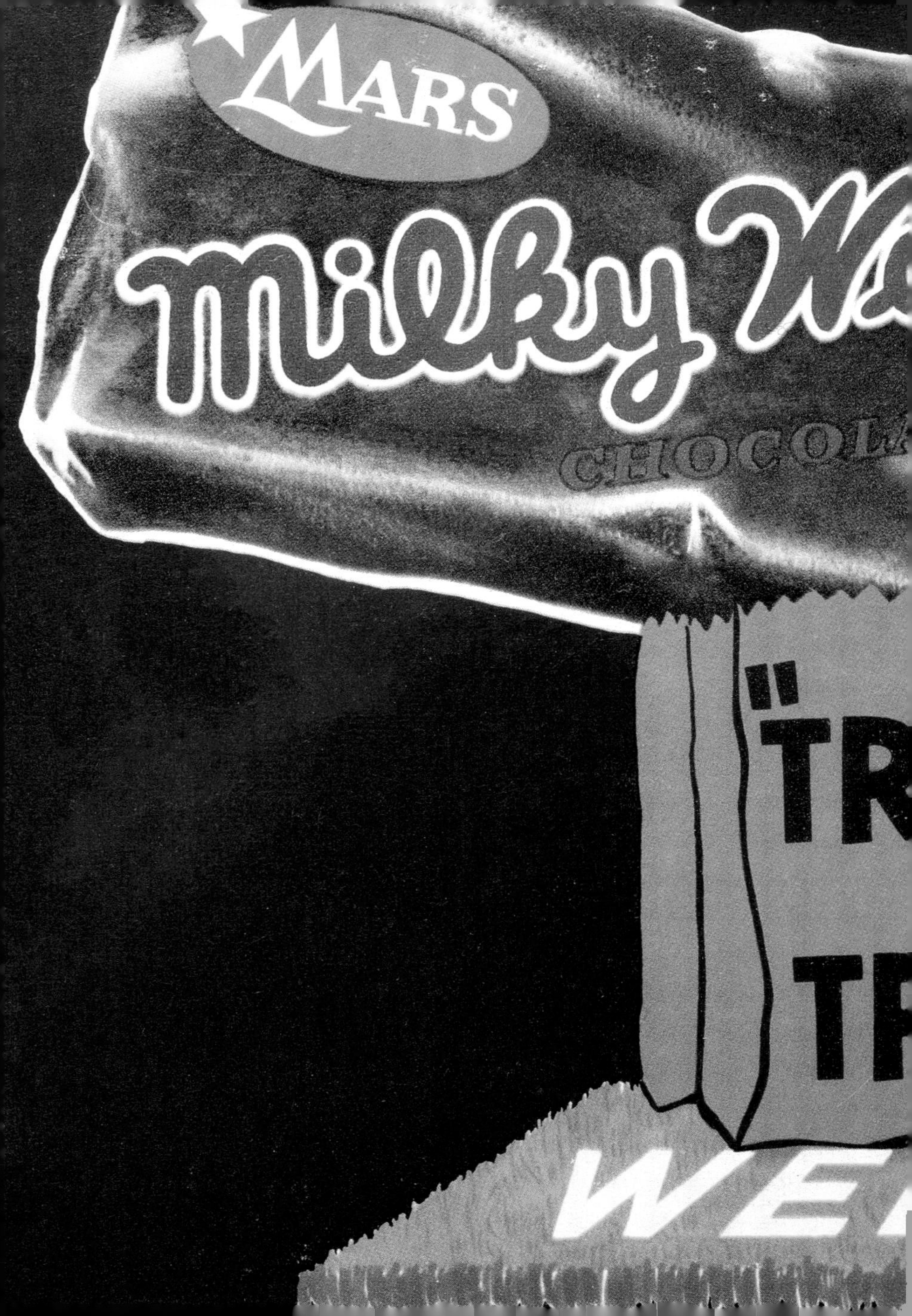
MARS

There is a maid for every man
And every man be free
At this last hour of halloween
By him to find the "She."

HALLOWEEN GREETINGS

When the Owl & Witch
to gether are seen,
There's mischief brewing
on HALLOWE'EN.

31

1944

A HALLOWE'EN WISH

ON HALLOWE'EN YOUR SLIGHTEST WISH
IS LIKELY TO COME TRUE,
SO BE CAREFUL, OR THE GOBELINS
WILL SPOIL YOUR WISH FOR YOU.

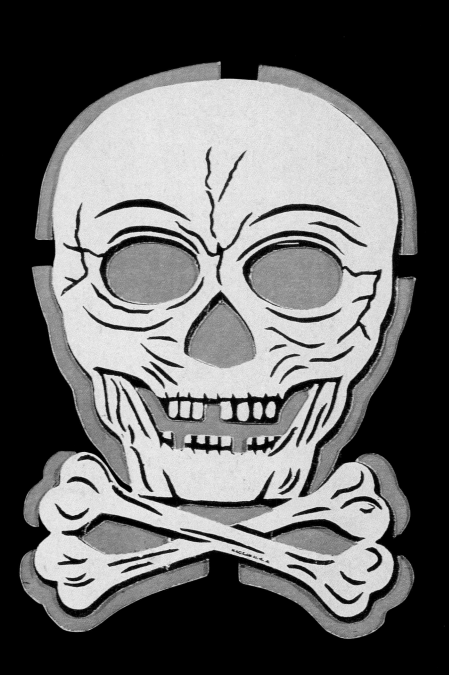

OCT 31st

ALL GOOD LUCK THIS HALLOWE'EN

trick or treat

masquerade costume

made of flame retardant material

Hallowe'en Greetings

THE WITCH

A. F. WEYMER CO.
SYRACUSE,
N. Y.

HALLOWE'EN

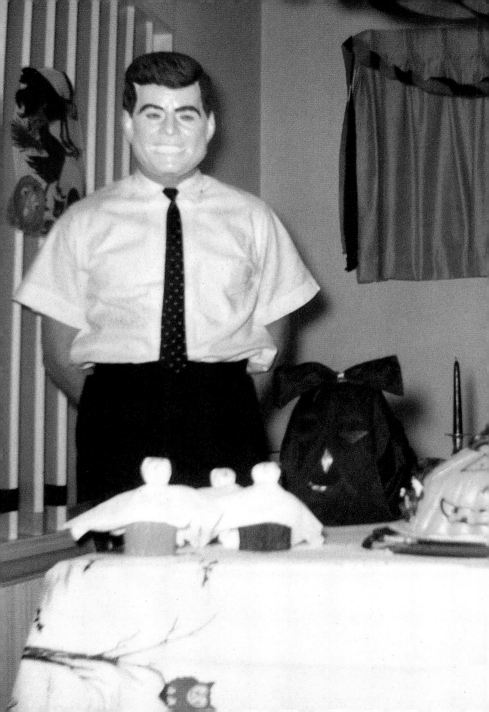

HALLOWE'EN TRIX or TREATS
(TRADE MARK)

I'm all dressed up, tonight's the night,
I wonder what people will say,
I'm not afraid, tho' it's dark and eerie
'Cause my pumpkin will light the way.

INGREDIENTS:
SUGAR, CORN SYRUP, CITRIC
ACID, U. S. CERTIFIED COLOR
ARTIFICIAL FLAVOR

MFD. FOR E. ROSEN COMPANY - PROVIDENCE. RHODE ISLAND - U. S. A.

HALLOWE'EN TRIX or TREATS
(TRADE MARK)

Did you ever see such a terrible sight
As this cat all ready to spring?
But tomorrow he'll be your same old pet,
The same sweet lovable thing.

INGREDIENTS:
SUGAR, CORN SYRUP, CITR
ACID, U. S. CERTIFIED COLC
ARTIFICIAL FLAVOR

MFD. FOR E. ROSEN COMPANY - PROVIDENCE, RHODE ISLAND - U. S

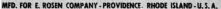

HALLOWE'EN TRIX or TREATS
(TRADE MARK)

The strangest things are out tonight,
To name them all I haven't room
The spookiest one of all I'd say
Was the witch I saw riding her broom.

INGREDIENTS
SUGAR, CORN SYRUP, CITRIC
ACID, U. S. CERTIFIED COLOR
ARTIFICIAL FLAVOR

MFD. FOR E. ROSEN COMPANY - PROVIDENCE, RHODE ISLAND - U. S. A.

HALLOWE'EN TRIX or TREATS
(TRADE MARK)

INGREDIENTS
SUGAR, CORN SYRUP, CITRIC
ACID, U. S. CERTIFIED COLOR
ARTIFICIAL FLAVOR

The ship's all ready - we're set to go
They think it's only a prank
But they'll change their minds, I'm telling you
When they have to walk the plank.

MFD. FOR E. ROSEN COMPANY - PROVIDENCE, RHODE ISLAND - U. S

THE LADIES' HOME JOURNAL

HALLOWE'EN GREETING

MADE IN U. S. A.

Copr H. E. Luhrs

73

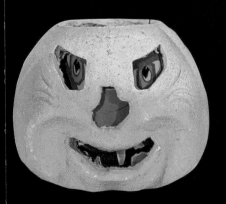
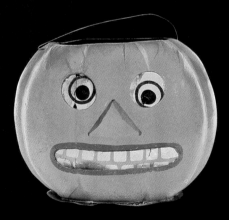

You're Invited!

F'
th
ir
th
p•

—

TRICK *that makes the* perfect TREAT – *anytime!*

or TREATS this Hallowe'en, Treat with Cracker Jack. It's a double
hat makes Hallowe'en twice as much fun. Every child gets a thrill
e surprise novelty that comes in every package. The second thrill is
l flavor of Cracker Jack. This famous crispy, crunchy, candy-coated
peanuts is childhood's favorite taste.

d for "Tricks or Treats" this Hallowe'en with plenty of Cracker Jack
ıy it by the case.

89

PRIZE
BRAND

HALLOWEEN COSTUME

RASCO
5-10-25¢ Stores
$1.00

WITH MASK • FLAME RETARDANT

Brach's Halloween Candy
for Trick or Treat

From Brach's candy kitchens comes exciting taste magic with these fascinating "Trick or Treat" candies. Skillfully created, colorfully packaged, Brach's "Trick or Treat" Halloween Candies are great to get—fun to give!

Please Come

HALLOWE'E

weet stalkin'!

n "TRICKS OR TREATS?" is the , here are two perfect answers: rs 6-Packs—Mars "24's". Better ht down to the store and get some.

6 of your favorite candy bars in one money-saving pack

MARS milky Way CHOCOLATE

MARS FAMILY CHOICE
SNICKERS
MARS
Forever Your
Cocoanut
6 ASSORTED BARS FROM
MARS
milky Way
MARS milky Way
CHOCOLATE
The answer to your taste question®

24 ★ MARS milk

ARS®

105

OCTOBER   1934

CHILD LIFE

The Children's Own Magazine

Frans
Kirn

In This Issue ~ RACHEL FIELD · BERTA AND ELMER HADER
DOROTHY LATHROP · LOIS LENSKI · KEITH WARD · AND OTHERS

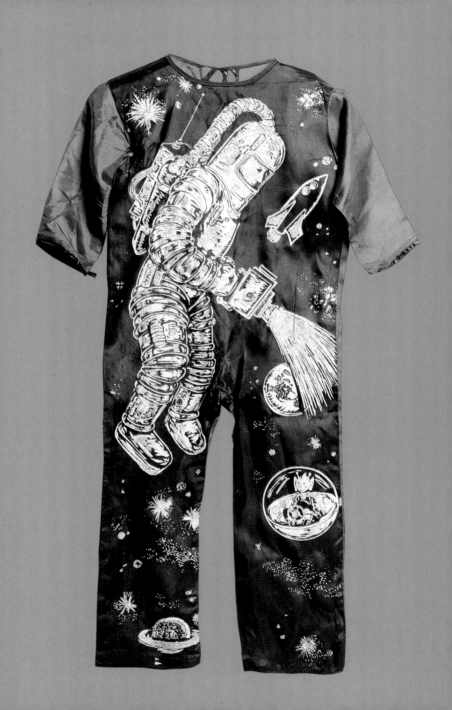

A HAPPY HALLOWE'EN

Ellen H. Clapsaddle

Hallowe'e

You would laugh too, if you had seen,
What the Moon saw, on HALLOWE'EN.

125

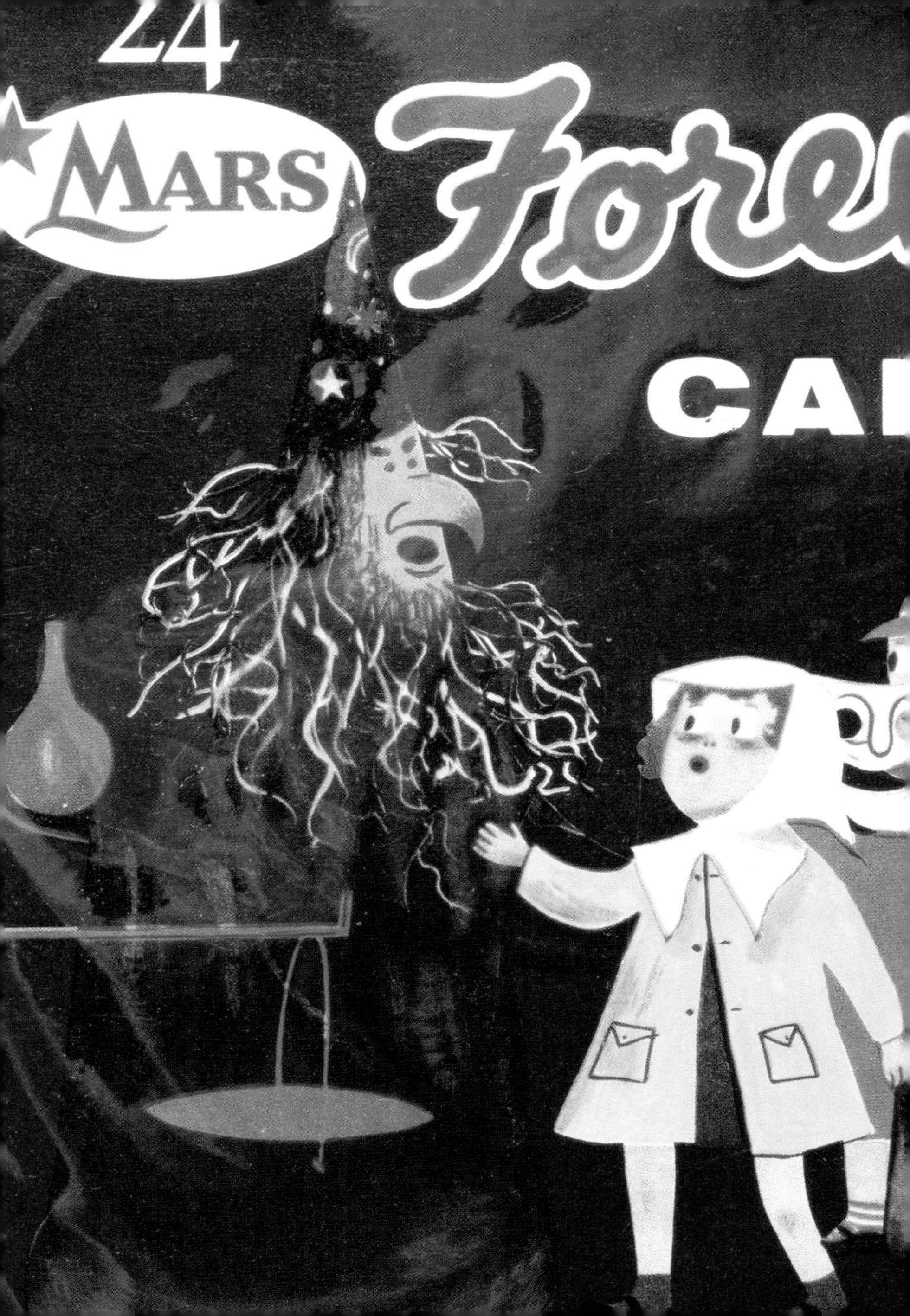
24
MARS
Fore
CA

Weeny Witch HALLOWEE

Party Book

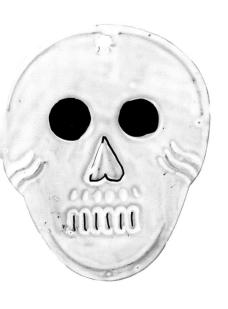

HALLOWEEN GREETING

TO MISS HALLOWEE E'N WITH YOU,
IS A THING, THAT I WOULD NEVER DO.

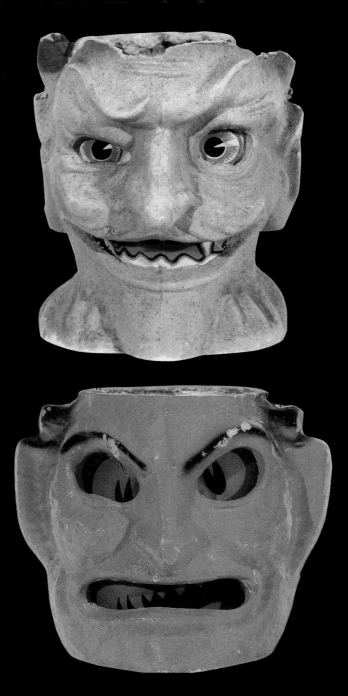

HALLOWE'EN GREETINGS

147

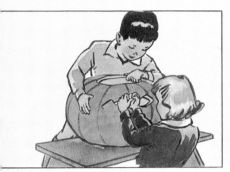

All Halloween

155

"Weeny Witch"

HALLOWEEN PARTY BOOK

FOR YOUR
HALLOWEEN
PARTY..SERVE..

B

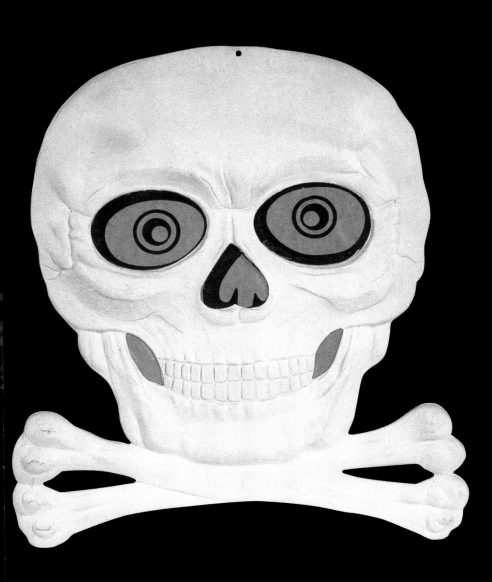

HALLOWEEN

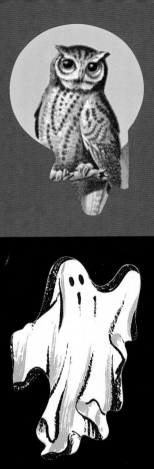

Jack-o'-Lantern

Words and music by Lillian E. Landman

Oh, Mis - ter Jack - o'-Lantern Man with your

eyes and mouth so wide,   Say, do you know you scare me so   I must

OCTOBER 1935

CHILD LIFE

The Children's Own Magazine

In This Issue — "THE BALKAN BURRO MYSTERY"
"JACK O'LANTERN" · "CROSS-WORD PUZZLE ·"
AND OTHER STORIES ·

MARIE LAWSON

TRICK'r TREAT

TRICK or TREAT

6 METAL COOKY CUTTERS•

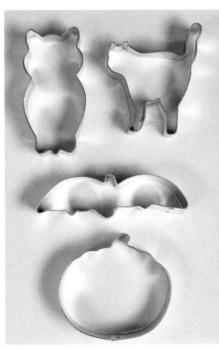

BAT

CAT

JACK O'LANTERN

DECORATING IDEAS

WITCH

OWL

BROOM

The Coca-Cola Company, Atlanta, Ga.

WHAT'S REALLY GOOD
FINDS ITS WAY EVERYWHERE

Forty years of public favor is but voluntary
recognition of its purity and wholesomeness
⸺ the delight in its refreshment.

IT HAD TO BE GOOD TO GET WHERE IT IS ⸺ 7 MILLION A DAY

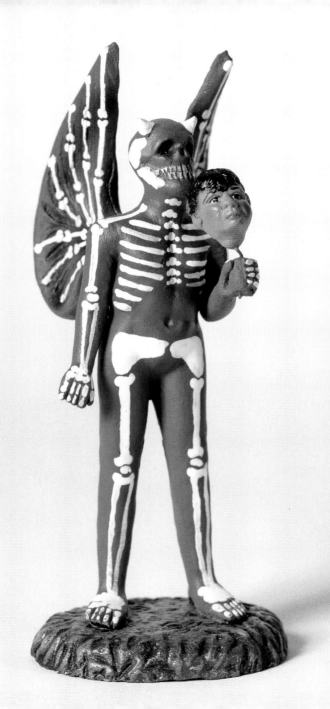

Collegeville Costumes

FLAME RETARDED

Acknowledgements

The ability to produce the Icon series with ease and speed is only possible with the help of a group of friends and colleagues whose interest, generosity, and enthusiasm make these projects a true joy. Among them are the ever important merchants of imagery who provided me with and loaned from their collections much of this book's content; Mel and Gary Baseman, Monte Beauchamp, Ralph Bowman, Dan and Ruth DePalma, Gary Fredericks, Dan Goodsell, Todd and Kathy Schorr, Bob Heitz, Martha Spelman, Julie Strnad, and Kirk Roberts.

On the TASCHEN side, author, scholar, and creative gadabout Steven Heller continues to produce our words with grace and gravity at a spooky pace while managing editor Nina Wiener, true to her organizational skills, keeps everything on course. Once again a bag full of candy corn to Cindy Vance for putting all the pieces together on the production side, and finally a bit of witches brew to our interns Alison Clarke and Vanessa Lopez for their professional help in gathering all the loose ends.

Any omissions for credit or copyright are unintentional and appropriate credit will be given in future editions if such copyright holders contact the publisher.

Front cover: Postcard, ca. 1928
Back cover: Greeting card, ca. 1936
Endpapers: Decoration, ca. 1940

© 2005 TASCHEN GmbH
Hohenzollernring 53, D–50672 Köln
www.taschen.com

Printed in Italy
ISBN 3-8228-4585-X

Editor & Art Direction: Jim Heimann, Los Angeles
Digital composition & Design: Cindy Vance,
Modern Art, Los Angeles
Production: Tina Ciborowius, Cologne
Project management: Florian Kobler and
Kathrin Murr, Cologne
English-language editor: Nina Wiener, Los Angeles
German translation: Anke Caroline Burger, Berlin
French translation: Lien, Amsterdam

★
ICONS